Tibetan Buddhism

To the world, Tibet and its form of Buddhism are shrouded in mystery and legend. Exploring beyond the merely exotic aspects of Tibetan Buddhism, this book offers a comprehensive overview that traces its history, demystifies its spiritual aspects and considers its future in the light of the present conditions.

TIBETAN BUDDHISM

An Introduction

SANGHARAKSHITA

New Age Books

ISBN: 978-81-7822-271-4

First Indian Edition: Delhi, 2010
This edition published by arrangement with
Windhorse Publications

Published by
NEW AGE BOOKS
A-44 Naraina Industrial Area, Phase-I
New Delhi (India)-110 028
Email: nab@vsnl.in
Website: www.newagebooksindia.com

For Sale in South Asia Only

Printed in India
at Shri Jainendra Press
A-45 Naraina Indl. Area, Phase-I, New Delhi-110 028

PUBLISHER'S NOTE

We at New Age Books have been bringing out books on a variety of subjects like Astrology, Ayurveda, Buddhism, Chakras, Chinese Therapics literature, Gita, Healing, Health Hinduism, Homeopathy, Inspiration Meditation, Music, Personal Growth, Philosophy, Psychology, Reiki, Religion, Spirituality, Tantra, Yoga etc. These books aim at helping individuals to grow in a rational, sensible and wise manner. Also to make a judicious combination of tradition and modernity and to make a holistic approach to all human issues and problems. So far we have brought out about 300 books. The response of our discerning readers has been quite encouraging.

We present this book as an essence of Tibetan Buddhism, a beautiful and noble tradition which can help us contact a sense of beauty and nobility of our lives.

Contents

Editor's Preface

In the mid-eighteenth century the Capuchin mission to Lhasa tried to win the souls of the people of Tibet for the Roman Catholic Church. The Tibetans showed an open-minded and tolerant interest in the Capuchins' faith, and at first the missionaries thought they were on fertile ground. However, after thirty years they had to admit to the Vatican that they had made only twenty-six converts, most of whom were their own household staff, and the mission was eventually abandoned. The Tibetan people remained staunchly Buddhist.

Over two centuries later, the spiritual map of the world is undergoing great changes. In many traditionally Buddhist countries, Buddhism is beleaguered by Westernization or – as in Tibet – by Communism. In the West, Christianity is in decline, and many people profess no religious faith at all.

However, since the Chinese invasion of Tibet, especially since the Lhasa uprising of 1959, the large exodus of refugees has brought many Tibetan Buddhist lamas and teachers to the West. Their approach to the Dharma is becoming widely known, alongside the many other Buddhist traditions that are spreading in the West. Buddhism is now one of the fastest growing religions in the Western world, offering a response to the spiritual yearning of many people who cannot go along with the dogmatism and blind faith of the religion of their upbringing, but who are also deeply dissatisfied with the merely secular and materialist values that pervade Western society.

Western interest in Tibet is not confined to Buddhists. In recent years people in the West have become increasingly aware of the gradual destruction of traditional Tibetan culture that has been taking place since the Chinese invasion, and of the plight of the Tibetan people under Chinese rule. But over and above political or humanitarian concerns, the Tibetans and their religion seem to hold a particular fascination for Westerners.

People often think of Tibet as a land shrouded in mystery and legend, and are intrigued by its form of Buddhism with its colourful symbolism and rituals. This fascination with Tibet has given rise to a plethora of books in the West about Tibetan Buddhism – its history, its doctrines, even its 'secret' Tantric practices. But the sheer range of information can lead to as much confusion as real understanding of Tibetan Buddhism. It is becoming difficult to see the wood for the trees, and to distinguish the essentials of Tibetan Buddhism from aspects that have more to do with Tibetan culture than with the Dharma. Western Buddhists need to be able to look beyond the merely exotic aspects of Tibetan Buddhism, to see what it truly has to offer to our own spiritual practice. As we embark on such a project, we need a succinct but comprehensive overview of the whole field, from which we can follow up particular interests in more detail. Such is the purpose of this book.

Sangharakshita is well placed to comment on Tibetan Buddhism. From 1950 until 1964 he lived in Kalimpong, a little town of about 15,000 inhabitants in Northern India, in the foothills of the Himalayas. Being close to the borders of several countries, Kalimpong is a meeting place of various races and religions. After the Chinese invasion of Tibet, many people who had fled from Tibet – including a number of eminent lamas – settled in and around Kalimpong. So from the mid-1950s onwards – a time when few Westerners had any knowledge of or interest in Tibetan Buddhism – Sangharakshita had close contact with refugee lamas of all schools.

The book is based on a series of lectures given by Sangharakshita in 1966, and therefore gives us his impressions of Tibetan Buddhism when he was quite fresh from his time in Kalimpong. In the mid-1960s he had returned to the UK, where in 1967 he founded the Friends of the Western Buddhist Order. Through this new Buddhist movement he has devoted himself to translating the traditional teachings and practices of

Buddhism into forms accessible to Westerners. This concern with translation was very much in evidence in these lectures. His account of Tibetan Buddhism clearly distinguishes what is essentially Buddhist from its cultural expression, but without losing sight of the particular beauty and flavour of the Tibetan approach.

When the lectures were given, Tibetan Buddhism was little known in the West, and Tibet itself was inaccessible. In addition to being under Chinese occupation, it was at that time suffering the additional horrors of the Cultural Revolution. Much has changed since then – Tibetan Buddhism is now quite well established in the West, and many Westerners have visited Tibet itself. Apart from some details of fact, no attempt has been made to update the content of the lectures, and the book should be read with this in mind. Often the present tense is used to describe a way of life which already belongs largely to the past.

In the first half of the book Sangharakshita acquaints us with Tibet and its people, and traces the history of the introduction of the Buddha's teaching into the land, showing that this was a protracted and difficult process. He outlines the four main schools of Tibetan Buddhism, summarizes their history and their general characteristics, and gives us some glimpses into the lives of their great founders – people like Padmasambhava, Milarepa, and Tsongkhapa. Discussion of the Gelug School leads to the subject of the Dalai Lama and what he represents for the Tibetan people. Sangharakshita then describes the traditional ways of life of monastic and lay Buddhists in Tibet, and explores their common bond, the Bodhisattva ideal.

The emphasis in the second four chapters is on the more spiritual aspects of Tibetan Buddhism. We are introduced to the symbolism of Tibetan Buddhist art and its religious function. Two chapters are devoted to Tibetan meditation practices, outlining the four foundation yogas, and clarifying what is involved in Tantric Buddhist meditation, which is well-known by reputation but little understood.

Having surveyed the remarkable past of Tibetan Buddhism, Sangharakshita then considers its future, in the light of the Chinese invasion and the flight of so many Tibetans into exile. Finally he outlines what we in the West can learn from Tibetan Buddhism. Tibetan Buddhism shows us what Indian Buddhism must have been like at the very height of its development. Buddhism had grown and flowered in India over a period of 1,500 years. Unfortunately it then died out in India itself, but before it did so it was imported almost in its entirety to the Land of Snows. Tibetan Buddhism therefore represents the culmination of fifteen centuries of

Indian Buddhism. This is why it is so important to a comprehensive understanding of the whole Buddhist tradition.

Now that all the major varieties of Eastern Buddhism have become known in the West, Sangharakshita stresses that we can derive inspiration from all of them. Rather than taking up any one form of oriental Buddhism to the exclusion of the others, we need to understand the essential teachings of all the varieties of Eastern Buddhism, and adapt them to our own requirements. This is how an indigenous form of Buddhism will gradually arise in Western countries. Western Buddhism will not be a carbon copy of Tibetan Buddhism, but it can learn a great deal from the Tibetan experience.

Several people assisted in bringing this book into being. I would particularly like to thank Vidyadevi for invaluable editorial advice and support. Most importantly I would like to acknowledge my profound gratitude to Sangharakshita, for all that he has done to create the conditions to facilitate the understanding and practice of the Buddha-Dharma in the West. It has been a great privilege for me to assist in bringing his lectures on Tibetan Buddhism to a wider audience.

Dharmacandra
Spoken Word Project
London
June 1996

ཨོཾ་མ་ཎི་པདྨེ་ཧཱུྃ། ཨོཾ་མ་ཎི་པདྨེ་ཧཱུྃ། ཨོཾ་མ་ཎི་པདྨེ་ཧཱུྃ།

ཨོཾ་མ་ཎི་པདྨེ་ཧཱུྃ། ཨོཾ་མ་ཎི་པདྨེ་ཧཱུྃ། ཨོཾ་མ་ཎི་པདྨེ་ཧཱུྃ།

1

How Buddhism came to Tibet

This is a story of special interest because of its sheer improbability. It is quite remarkable that Buddhism should have come from India to Tibet at all. We are accustomed to thinking of Tibet as a Buddhist country, perhaps *the* Buddhist country. But it wasn't always such. Before it actually happened, the chances that Buddhism might ever be transplanted from India to the Land of Snows must have appeared pretty remote.

India and Tibet may be very close as the crow flies, but they are in fact worlds apart. Between them there is a tremendous barrier: the Himalayas. This colossal mountain range extends roughly 2,000 miles, dividing India, on the southern side, from Tibet in the north. The two countries are therefore virtually cut off from each other. They are also divided climatically. India's climate is subtropical, characterized by blazing hot sunshine, torrential monsoon rains, and periods of drought. Tibet, on the other hand, at 12,000 feet above sea-level, has clear skies, a bracing atmosphere, and temperatures that are often well below freezing point.

With different climates we find different ways of life. India was, and still is, a predominantly agricultural country. The land has been cultivated for centuries, and its people enjoy a settled, placid existence in thousands of little villages. But in Tibet the economy was mainly pastoral. People kept great flocks of sheep and herds of yaks, and followed a nomadic way of life, wandering all over the vast open spaces, living in tents and on horseback. Indians and Tibetans also belong to quite different ethnic groups. India is inhabited by a mixture of the predominantly Aryan peoples of the north and the Dravidians of the south, while the Tibetans belong to a sub-group of the Mongolian peoples which also includes the Burmese and the Newars of Nepal.

All these factors are reflected in the marked differences of temperament which exist between Indians and Tibetans. At the risk of over-generalizing, I would say that Indians tend to be rather mystical, in the broadest sense of the term. They are very aware of the presence of a higher spiritual world or transcendental dimension. If you happen to meet someone in India, say on a bus or train or simply walking along the road, you can very quickly strike up a conversation about things of a religious or mystical nature. This is the sort of language Indians understand, the sort of outlook they accept and, in a sense, take for granted. Where practical matters are concerned, they can sometimes be rather vague and uncomprehending, but speak to them in terms of ultimate reality and they will know at once what you are talking about.

The Tibetan character is quite different. In the West we like to think of Tibetans as mysterious, exotic, other-worldly people. We imagine that when they are not levitating or flying through the air they are busy opening their third eye. But in reality they are not like this at all. From my experience of living among the Tibetans of Kalimpong, I would say that there are no people on earth more practical. They are hard-headed businessmen; even the monks know how to handle complex business transactions. And when it comes to practical tasks, even if they have not done something before they will study it, find out all about it, and puzzle out the secret of how to do it. Tibetans coming to India often made good motor mechanics; in fact they take well to anything of a mechanical nature. So whereas Indians are rather mystical, with their heads in the clouds (the Sikhs are an exception to this), Tibetans are very practical, with their feet firmly on the ground. Tibetans also have this practical, down-to-earth approach when it comes to the religious life, as we shall see in subsequent chapters.

Then again Indians, especially Hindus, are generally peaceable people. As individuals, at least, they don't like getting into a fight. In India a dispute in the street usually remains verbal. The disputants may scream at each other, they may dance around each other in a rage, and perhaps even go so far as to pull one another's hair, but they are very unlikely to come to blows. Tibetans, on the other hand, tend to be warlike and aggressive, even swashbuckling. In Kalimpong some of the refugees used to strut around as though they had conquered the place. Many of them wore short swords, and they would swagger along the road, shouldering any Indians who happened to get in their way roughly aside, sometimes sending them flying. People learned to be wary of the Tibetans, especially of the Khampas of eastern Tibet.

I used to teach English to Tibetan students in Kalimpong, and I sometimes gave them an exercise in which they had to complete a sentence like 'I ... my brother,' filling in the blank with a suitable verb. In nine cases out of ten they would come up with 'I *killed* my brother.' A Nepalese friend of mine, who was the police surgeon and worked in the local hospital, told me that every week he had to deal with at least two cases of stabbing from within the Tibetan community, which at that time numbered about 2,000. Occasionally the stabbings were fatal.

In my experience Tibetan Buddhists are thus quite a fierce people, quite rough at the edges, so to speak. Indians are rather more gentle and refined. Even those leading a materially simple rural existence are often more truly cultured than many Westerners. Tibetans, by comparison, I found to be on the whole rather unpolished, though members of the Lhasa aristocracy could be very sophisticated indeed.

When Indian Buddhism came to Tibet, it therefore encountered a completely different culture and way of life. Of course, when the Buddha gained Enlightenment, he rose above all distinctions of race and nationality. What he had reached, what he had realized, was something purely spiritual, something transcendental. Historically speaking, however, Buddhism is a product of markedly Indian origin, reflecting Indian modes of thought, Indian cultural attitudes and assumptions. For instance, when we read Indian Buddhist texts, especially the great Mahāyāna sūtras, we encounter the characteristically Indian tendency to exaggerate. If a story is being told, say about a woman who had so many children, the story might begin by saying that she had a dozen children; but then, not content to leave it at that, the author will go on to say that she had twenty children, or even fifty or a hundred. This kind of exaggeration is typically Indian.

In view of the vast differences between the Indian and Tibetan people, and the fact that after fifteen hundred years in India Buddhism possessed many typically Indian characteristics, one might have thought that Indian Buddhism was the last religion the Tibetans would choose to adopt. But, strange as it may seem, they did choose it. It took them, however, a very long time, a fact which is not always appreciated. It was not that one day someone went from India to Tibet and preached Buddhism, and then a few years later the Tibetans were all Buddhists. The Tibetans, especially the Tibetan nobles, put up considerable resistance, and the establishment of Buddhism as the religion of Tibet was a long and sometimes difficult process.

Perhaps we in the West can derive some comfort from this. We might think that things here are moving pretty slowly. Buddhism has been known in the West for about a century, yet we do not seem to have got very far with it. But in the case of Tibet it took very much longer. In fact the mere introduction of Buddhism into Tibet took approximately 500 years – much longer than it took, for example, to introduce Christianity into Britain. The 500-year period in question, from the seventh to the eleventh centuries CE, was a time of constant political upheaval. This was no coincidence, much of the upheaval being directly connected with the introduction of Buddhism.

In the East at that time – as in the West – the predominant form of government was absolute monarchy. (Throughout the East, wherever Buddhism spread, it did so under the patronage of powerful kings.) This is true of India, where Buddhism was given a great impetus by the emperor Aśoka, it is true of China and Japan, and it is also true of Tibet. The introduction of Buddhism into Tibet was associated particularly with four *dharmarājas*, or religious kings, and with the Buddhist monks and scholars, both Indian and Tibetan, with whom these kings collaborated. The first three of these kings ruled over the whole of Tibet, and the fourth was a king of western Tibet after the country had split up into a number of independent states.

The first religious king of Tibet was Songtsen Gampo, who ruled in the seventh century, and seems to have been a remarkable man. His earliest achievement consisted in continuing the political and administrative reforms initiated by his father. Until that time, Tibet had been split into a number of different feudal principalities, but Songtsen Gampo – and his father before him – gradually brought them all together, centralizing the administration and establishing Tibet as a single political unit with a military power which was greatly feared by all her neighbours.

This was itself a great achievement, but it was not enough for Songtsen Gampo. At that time Tibet was surrounded by a number of highly civilized states: Khotan to the north-west; Kashmir (then an independent kingdom) to the west; Nepal to the south-west (and beyond Nepal, of course, India); and the great empire of China, then under the T'ang emperors, to the east. All these states were Buddhist in those days, and all of them had attained a very high level of civilization and culture. Songtsen Gampo could not help noticing this. He saw that although Tibet was politically united and in military terms a force to be reckoned with, where civilization and culture were concerned she very much lagged behind all her neighbours.

So Songtsen Gampo embarked on a programme of social reform and cultural development. First he redistributed the land that was in the possession of the nobles and great landowners, to give the common people a bigger and better share. At the same time he encouraged agriculture, trying to persuade the wandering nomadic tribes to settle down and cultivate the soil. He introduced weaving, masonry, and carpentry. He also decided to prohibit blood sports, a step which hints at the beginnings of his sympathy with Buddhism. Another old custom he prohibited was that of face-painting. Apparently Tibetans, men and women alike, had a custom of painting their faces bright red, but Songsten Gampo outlawed this, thinking it rather uncivilized.

In the course of his travels and military campaigns Songtsen Gampo had observed that the culture of the surrounding countries was very closely linked with Buddhism, and this led him to decide that Buddhism should be introduced in Tibet. He was supported in this mission by his two principal wives, the daughter of the king of Nepal, and the daughter of the emperor of China. What might have happened if the king's wives had followed religions other than Buddhism is an open question, but fortunately both were devout Buddhists. In Tibetan art they are often depicted on either side of Songtsen Gampo.

For his Nepalese wife, Songtsen Gampo built the Jokhang, literally 'Lord's House', in Lhasa. European writers often call it the 'Cathedral of Lhasa'. It is the oldest religious building in the Tibetan capital, and the one the Tibetans consider the most sacred. For his Chinese wife he built a smaller temple known as the Ramoche. In these temples were installed images of Akṣobhya and Śākyamuni brought from their respective countries by his wives. The temples were desecrated and demolished by the Chinese during the Cultural Revolution. Devout Tibetans later surreptitiously removed the battered heads of these two great images, which had been there for thirteen centuries, and brought them to India, where they presented them to the Dalai Lama. They were made of a sort of painted stucco, quite easily damaged, and I remember that many Indians were deeply affected by the photographs of them in the newspapers.

During the course of his reign, Songtsen Gampo built many other temples, the first Buddhist temples to be built in Tibet. He also sent a group of young Tibetans to study Buddhism in Kashmir, which in those days had a reputation for Buddhist learning. But such were the rigours of the climate (Kashmir being decidedly hot compared to Tibet, even though it is cool compared to the rest of India) that only one of the party survived to return to Tibet. This was the celebrated Tönmi Sambhota, who invented the Tibetan alphabet in around 632CE. Before that time the Tibetans had no script and therefore, of course, no literature. Tönmi Sambhota devised the Tibetan alphabet on the basis of one of the Indian scripts, probably the Sharada script, with which he had become familiar during his sojourn in Kashmir, and the first Tibetan translations of Indian Buddhist scriptures began to be made. According to tradition, the very first text to be translated was the *Maṇi Kabum*. *Maṇi* here refers to the *oṁ maṇi padme hūṁ* mantra, and *kabum* means 100,000 words, the text being a sort of encyclopaedia about the mantra – how it originated, what it means, how it should be recited, and so on. Paper and ink for printing were also introduced from China at this time, as well as painting and sculpture.

Thus Songtsen Gampo practically created Tibetan culture, at least in its rudimentary form. Furthermore, he caused a new code of civil law to be drafted, and he ensured that the ethical precepts of Buddhism were widely taught throughout his domain. But as yet there were no Buddhist monks or monasteries in Tibet. In fact, Songtsen Gampo's interest in Buddhism appears to have been more cultural than religious. This was inevitable, given the state of Tibet in those days. The spiritual life can develop only when a certain standard of culture – in the sense not of material improvement but of the refinement of one's whole way of life – has been attained. But, even with this very important reservation, Songtsen Gampo's work remains of the first importance. He laid the foundations of the Tibetan nation, of its culture and literature, and of Tibetan Buddhism itself – surely a very considerable achievement for one man. The Tibetans show their gratitude to Songtsen Gampo even to this day by regarding him as a manifestation of the great Bodhisattva of Compassion, Avalokiteśvara (the Dalai Lama being another, later, one).

Songtsen Gampo's work did not come to an end when he died. More and more texts were translated from Indian languages into Tibetan. Monks started coming from neighbouring countries, including refugees from Khotan where Buddhists were being persecuted, and even put to the sword, by the Muslim hordes that were beginning to sweep across Central Asia. At the same time, there was growing opposition to Buddhism in Tibet itself amongst the followers of the indigenous religion, Bön. This opposition stemmed mainly from noble families who resented the growing power and prestige of the Buddhist monarchy, and also the Bön priests who no doubt felt that their livelihood was under threat.

The second religious king of Tibet, Trisong Detsen, lived in the eighth century. He was an ardent supporter of Buddhism, but during the earlier part of his reign he was greatly hampered by the hostility of the followers of Bön. He invited to Tibet the Indian scholar and teacher Śantarakṣita, best known nowadays as the author of a great work of Mahāyāna Buddhist philosophy called the *Tattvasaṅgraha*. But unfortunately Śantarakṣita's mission was not very successful. He visited several places, he spoke on Buddhism, he gave a number of lectures, but then apparently an epidemic broke out all over the country. This gave the Bönists the opportunity they had been waiting for. They said, 'You see what happens. In comes this Indian Buddhist teacher, and there is an epidemic! The demons are angry.' Śantarakṣita could find no answer for this, and knew another approach was needed. He advised the king to invite to Tibet the great Indian master Padmasambhava, who was then living at Nalanda University near Bodh Gaya.

Padmasambhava is one of the most remarkable figures in the entire history of Buddhism. Not only was he a great scholar and an accomplished debater and philosopher; he was also a formidable yogi, a great meditator, and a mystic. He was a great master of the occult sciences, and according to tradition he was also a magician to be reckoned with. He spent only eighteen months in Tibet, but during that time he brought the Bön 'demons' under control. Tradition tells us that he incorporated the lot of them, willy-nilly, into the Tantric Buddhist pantheon, converting them into guardian deities of the Buddhist faith.

We should not dismiss stories of this kind as mere legendary accretions to the historical facts. The story has a profound psychological and spiritual significance. After all, what is Bön? What does it represent? Broadly speaking, it is the indigenous shamanistic religion of Tibet, and like all forms of shamanism it is very closely connected with the psyche of the people practising it. One may go so far as to say that the Bön deities or 'demons' are in a sense archetypes of the Tibetan collective unconscious. Thus their hostility to Buddhism, in the traditional account, can be said to represent the unconscious resistance of the Tibetan psyche to the higher and more spiritual ideals of Buddhism. The Tibetans could not take them in all at once. The Tibetan mind was, after all, very different from the Indian mind. It therefore put up resistance, and this is symbolized on the archetypal level by the resistance and hostility of the Bön deities who created the epidemic.

Śantarakṣita was a very great man, but he had his limitations. As a scholar, a philosopher, he could appeal to the conscious mind of the Tibetans, but he did not have the resources to overcome their unconscious resistance to Buddhist ideals. Padmasambhava, on the other hand, was not just a great scholar, not just an eminent philosopher; he was also a yogi and mystic, which meant that he could break through to a deeper level and make contact with the forces operating within the Tibetan collective unconscious. He was able to incorporate the Bön deities and the forces they represented into the framework of Buddhism, and even to use the energy contained in these archetypes in the interests of the spiritual life.

The Bön demons having been 'converted', Padmasambhava and Śantarakṣita together founded the first monastery in Tibet, Samye, in 779CE. Built after the model of the famous Odantapuri Monastery in India, Samye was completed in the year 787CE. Much of it was recently destroyed by the Chinese, but a film of it made by the Indian representative in Lhasa before the desecration shows that it was a very beautiful place, reminiscent of what the great ancient Indian monastic universities must have looked like in their heyday. Śantarakṣita and Padmasambhava also ordained seven Tibetans as monks, thus founding the Tibetan monastic Sangha.

Padmasambhava left a permanent mark on Tibetan Buddhism, through the sheer force of his personality. Although he only stayed in Tibet for about eighteen months, the Tibetan accounts of his visit usually make out that it lasted for thirty-five years, presumably because he created such an impact in those eighteen months that it was as though he had been there for thirty-five years. He is traditionally regarded as the founder of the Nyingma School, but he is greatly revered by the followers of all sects and schools of Tibetan Buddhism. If you go into practically any Tibetan Buddhist temple you will see an image or picture of the great guru Padmasambhava.

It is a very distinctive image, so much so that one can readily believe it represents him as he appeared in life, because the details are always the same. He is a tall well-built Indian, in the prime of life, with the faintly Mongoloid features characteristic of the people of East Bengal. He has a drooping moustache and a little beard, and a hint of ferocity in his expression. He is dressed in princely robes and wears a lotus cap with a vulture's feather on the top. Sometimes he carries a skull-cup filled with blood, sometimes a dagger, and sometimes the *dorje*, the diamond-thunderbolt. In the crook of his arm is a staff surmounted by three skulls (the *khatvanga*). The images convey an impression of a remarkable figure, a supremely lively, virile, active, and powerful person. You can't mistake Padmasambhava for anyone else.

Another highly significant event during Trisong Detsen's reign was what Western scholars usually call the 'Council of Lhasa', although it was in fact more of a debate than a council, and it took place at Samye. The debate was between Kamalaśīla, one of Śantarakṣita's Indian disciples, and a Chinese monk who had turned up in Tibet and was preaching Ch'an (the Chinese forerunner of Japanese Zen) to the disapproval of some Tibetan Buddhists. So in 792CE a discussion was arranged between Kamalaśīla and the Ch'an monk. We still have detailed records of this event, and the chief point of contention, apparently, was over the question of whether Enlightenment came gradually, little by little, or occurred all at once, in a great rush. Following the general Indian tradition, the Indian scholar held that it came gradually, step by step, by following the Eightfold Path, practising the ten *pāramitās*, and so on; while the Chinese monk argued that it happened all at once.

The debate was adjudicated by King Trisong Detsen, and he decided in favour of Kamalasila. However, those who have studied the records believe that the Chinese Ch'an master did pretty well too. Looking at it quite objectively and impartially, one might say that the point at issue between them is really a distinction without a difference. One does not attain Enlightenment either slowly or quickly; ultimately the question of time does not come into it at all. But the king said that Kamalaśīla had won, and that was that.

Trisong Detsen further decreed that from then on Tibetan Buddhists should follow the Sarvāstivāda School (one of the main Hīnayāna schools) with respect to vinaya or religious discipline, the Mādhyamika and Yogācāra Schools of the Mahāyāna for their philosophy and metaphysics, and the Tantra, the Vajrayāna, as far as meditation was concerned. In this way a synthesis of the three yānas was established. These three aspects of practice were also conceived of as constituting successive stages of the spiritual path. First you follow Sarvāstivāda discipline, then you study Mādhyamika and Yogācāra philosophy, and then you practise Tantric meditation; in this way your spiritual life is complete. Thus the reign of Trisong Detsen saw three main developments: interest in Buddhism shifted from the cultural to the religious; the monastic order was established; and the triyāna character of Tibetan Buddhism was determined.

The third religious king of Tibet was Ralpachen, who reigned in the ninth century. He was an even more ardent Buddhist than Trisong Detsen, and did a great deal for the propagation of Buddhism. He established more temples and monasteries, he encouraged Buddhist arts and crafts, and perhaps most important of all, he set up a permanent commission for the translation of the scriptures. This meant that you could not just learn Sanskrit if you felt like it and translate a Buddhist text into Tibetan; you had to get permission from this commission, which laid down rules of translation. It compiled a glossary (which still exists) of Buddhist terms in Sanskrit and Tibetan, and in this way the translation of Buddhist scriptures into Tibetan was made regular and uniform. For example, the commission decided that the Sanskrit word 'Dharma' was to be translated *chos*, and nobody was allowed to translate it any other way. This decision meant that the Tibetans did not come up against the sort of obstacle which English-speaking students of Buddhism have to deal with. When you read *chos* in a Tibetan text you know that it means 'Dharma'; but in English translations Dharma is sometimes translated as 'Law', sometimes as 'Doctrine', sometimes as 'Truth', sometimes as 'Norm'. Beginners hardly know where they are, because the same word is rendered in so many different ways by different translators. By compiling a glossary which everyone had to follow, the Tibetan commission prevented this sort of confusion, thus making way for the effective study of Buddhism.

Unfortunately, in the midst of these advances, King Ralpachen was assassinated as a result of a Bön conspiracy, and was succeeded, in 836CE, by his brother Langdarma, who was completely opposed to Buddhism. A period of persecution ensued. Buddhist temples and monasteries were demolished, monks were killed or driven out, scriptures were destroyed, and the result was that Buddhism practically perished in Tibet, especially in central Tibet, for nearly two centuries. Only a few faithful followers kept the flame of the Dharma alive in those dark days.

It was a time of great political upheaval, and eventually the country broke up into a number of different states. It was also a period of religious confusion. Hindu Tantric teachers infiltrated Tibet from Kashmir with some very questionable practices that began to give the Tantra a bad name. Even Buddhism itself, as much of it as had survived in Tibet, became more and more debased and corrupt, and this was a source of serious concern to a number of earnest Buddhists. When things quietened down a little they decided, under the protection of the fourth religious king, Yeshe Ö, to invite to Tibet the great teacher Atīśa from

Vikramaśīla, another of the great monastic universities of north-eastern India.

Yeshe Ö was king of western Tibet in the eleventh century. Buddhism had fared rather better here during the period of persecution, and Yeshe Ö did much, within the boundaries of his own kingdom, to revive and propagate it. He even took the step of becoming a monk himself. His fortunes then took an even more dramatic turn. Towards the end of his life he went on an expedition to collect from his subjects the huge quantity of gold needed to fetch Atīśa from India. But in the course of his journey he was captured by a neighbouring Muslim king who gave him an ultimatum. He should either become a Muslim or be ransomed for his own weight in gold.

It was, of course, out of the question for Yeshe Ö to become a Muslim. But where was the ransom to come from? The king's nephew was very devoted to him and resolved to collect as much gold as he possibly could, but even in a gold-bearing country like Tibet it's not easy to collect the weight of a man in gold. Over the months, over the years, he gradually amassed a large quantity. But when he finally visited the king in the dungeon where he had been kept all those years, he found that he had only enough gold to weigh against his uncle's body, not against his head as well. So he said 'What shall I do? Shall I make a last effort to get more gold?' But the king said, 'I'm a very old man, and I have not yet had the opportunity to sacrifice my life for the Dharma. Don't bother about me any more. Don't give the gold to my captors. Use it instead to bring Atīśa to Tibet.' So this was what was done, and when the Muslim king realized that no gold was going to be forthcoming, Yeshe Ö was murdered.

So Atīśa, the greatest Buddhist teacher in India at that time, came to Tibet, and stayed there for twelve years, until his death. He worked hard and accomplished a great deal. He reformed the monastic discipline, he purified the practice of the Tantra, he laid the foundations for the Kadam School, and he wrote a number of works for the spiritual guidance of the Tibetans. Largely as a result of Atīśa's influence, there ensued a tremendous revival of Buddhism in Tibet. Before the end of the eleventh century Marpa and Milarepa had initiated the Kagyu lineage, and Könchok Gyelpo had founded the Sakya School. After so many struggles, ups and downs, reverses and successes, Buddhism was at last (by the time of the Norman conquest in England) finally established in Tibet. From then onwards it was never seriously challenged as the dominant religion until the invasion in the 1950s by communist China.

ཨོཾ་མ་ཎི་པདྨེ་ཧཱུྃ། ཨོཾ་མ་ཎི་པདྨེ་ཧཱུྃ། ཨོཾ་མ་ཎི་པདྨེ་ཧཱུྃ།

ཨོཾ་མ་ཎི་པདྨེ་ཧཱུྃ། ཨོཾ་མ་ཎི་པདྨེ་ཧཱུྃ། ཨོཾ་མ་ཎི་པདྨེ་ཧཱུྃ།

2

The Schools of Tibetan Buddhism

Tibetan Buddhism is divided, broadly speaking, into four major schools, but as the term 'school' could be misleading we need to be clear about what it means in this context. I have chosen to use the word 'school' in preference to 'sect', which has a rather negative connotation. We might equally speak of the four major 'traditions' of Tibetan Buddhism. None of these English words, however, is completely satisfactory. We usually think of the sects or schools of any religion as being mutually exclusive in membership and doctrine; if you belong to one, you cannot belong to another, and what one of them teaches may even contradict the teaching of another. But it is not like that in Buddhism, not in Tibetan Buddhism, nor in Indian Buddhism, which provided the pattern for the Tibetan tradition.

To trace the rise and fall, the development and the flowering, of the different schools of the Indian Buddhist tradition is very difficult. The lines of transmission continually overlap and flow into one another, so that you can never identify any particular school very clearly or definitively. It keeps shading off into another school – or even into several. In the Western religious context we are accustomed to sharp divisions. If we look at the history of the Christian churches down the centuries, we can say quite definitely that someone was either, say, Roman Catholic or

Methodist or Baptist. These are all clear-cut divisions. But Indian Buddhism is not sectarian. Schools exist, but they are not very sharply defined, so that in the case of certain great teachers, they cannot be definitely identified with one particular school more than with another. There is a dispute, for example, as to whether Maitreyanātha, the great author of the Five Treatises, was a Mādhyamika or a Yogācārin. It is very difficult to say, because his works strike such a beautiful balance between these two viewpoints.

Tibetan Buddhism follows this Indian non-sectarian pattern. So if we ask ourselves what is meant by a 'school' of Tibetan Buddhism, all we can say is that it is a particular lineage of teachers and disciples. A certain teacher teaches Buddhism to his disciples, they teach their disciples, and so on. This succession from master to pupils, who become masters in their turn and teach their own pupils, is what we call the school. The line of transmission may have its own angle on the Dharma, it may stress a particular aspect of the doctrine or a particular practice, but the emphasis is no more than an emphasis. Rarely, if ever, is it exclusive.

Sometimes a certain line of teachers and pupils may be associated with a particular monastery. This is usually quite fortuitous; the teacher happens to live in a certain monastery to which his disciples come, and when the original teacher dies his pupils stay on and teach there. Thus the monastery comes to be associated with a certain line of transmission and may become the 'headquarters' of that school.

Sometimes too a certain school, or line of teachers, may be associated with a particular group of texts. The Buddhist scriptures are voluminous, and it is not easy – indeed not possible – for one person to study them all even in a cursory manner. We therefore find in the history of Buddhism a sort of division of labour whereby a particular line of teachers and disciples concentrates on the study, the explication, and even the propagation, of a specific group of texts. Again, this is one of the ways in which a school arises. It is as if a particular group of Christians were to take up, say, the study of St John's Gospel and were to concentrate on studying, teaching, and writing commentaries only on that text, thus becoming a school of teachers and pupils devoted exclusively to it – though without detriment to their respect for the rest of the Bible. This has never happened in the case of Christianity, but it is the sort of thing that happens very often in Buddhism. Chinese Buddhist schools, especially, tend to be associated with a particular scriptural text or group of texts; the T'ien T'ai School, for instance, concentrates on the *Saddharma-puṇḍarīka Sūtra*, the 'Sūtra of the White Lotus of the Good Law'.

Then again, schools sometimes arise because a certain line of teachers and pupils is associated with a particular type of spiritual practice, especially a particular type of meditation. The teacher has practised a certain kind of meditation, he teaches it to his pupils, and in this way a line is established which may become the nucleus of a school.

The birth of a school may involve several such factors combined together. Over time, each school assumes a more and more distinctive character, but without ever becoming exclusive. In keeping with the tolerant spirit of Buddhism, no school of Tibetan Buddhism claims to teach the one true version of the Dharma. Differences are recognized, they are not glossed over, but no school would go so far as to maintain that it had a monopoly of Buddhist truth.

In chronological order, the four major schools of Tibetan Buddhism are: the Nyingma School, the Kagyu School, the Sakya School, and the Gelug School. The first three are known as the old schools, and the Gelug is called the new school. Sometimes the first three are called the unreformed schools and the Gelug the reformed school, but some Tibetan Buddhists contend that this distinction is not quite fair. I once discussed this with a very eminent Nyingma lama. I asked him, 'What is the basis for this classification? How is it that you and the Kagyupas and Sakyapas are called unreformed whereas the Gelugpas are known as reformed?' (The suffix *-pa* means simply 'man' or 'person'.)He just smiled and said, 'We didn't need to be reformed.'

Western scholars tend to regard the three old schools as unreformed much as they regard the Roman Catholic Church as unreformed compared to the Protestant churches, but this analogy is not very helpful. In fact, the major difference between them is that the three old schools are of directly Indian origin, having been founded either by Indians or by Tibetans who had studied in India. But the Gelug School, the new school, is indigenous in the sense that Tsongkhapa, its founder, never went outside Tibet. The school which he founded is of purely Tibetan origin.

Before we look at the four schools individually, we should note some of their common characteristics. Firstly, the Buddhism of all these schools is *triyāna* in character. To understand this term, one needs to understand something of the history of Indian Buddhism. Buddhism lasted for about 1,500 years in India, from about 500BCE to 1000CE, and passed through three clearly marked stages during each of which particular aspects were predominant.

The first stage, which lasted for some 500 years, was marked by a predominantly ethical and psychological emphasis in the way the

Dharma was expounded. There was a great deal of close study and analysis of the mind, especially in connection with meditation and higher states of consciousness. There was also a strong emphasis on ethical discipline and monastic rules. This first stage in the development of Indian Buddhism is therefore often described as the ethico-psychological phase.

The second stage developed and emphasized two additional elements: the metaphysical and the devotional. There was no rejection of the ethical and psychological, but while that tradition was continued, the nature of Reality was explored more deeply in conceptual terms. At the same time much more stress was placed on the importance of the devotional element in Buddhism, the importance of the worship of the Buddhas and Bodhisattvas and of the emotions of reverence, love, and respect. This metaphysical-devotional phase in the development of Indian Buddhism also lasted about 500 years.

During the third stage, from approximately 500CE to 1000CE, the ethico-psychological and the metaphysical-devotional traditions were continued, but the emphasis again shifted. It came to be placed more and more on the performance of ritual acts and procedures with certain archetypal meanings and values, and also on what we can only describe as 'esoteric meditation'. This is not ordinary concentration of mind, but advanced meditation which may be practised only under the personal guidance of a guru after the proper initiation or empowerment, about which more is said in Chapter 7.

In traditional Buddhist language each of these three stages of development is called a *yāna*, which means 'path' or 'way', and is also sometimes translated as 'vehicle', in the sense of a vehicle for spiritual practice and progress. So the Sanskrit term *triyāna* refers to these three phases of Indian Buddhism: the Hīnayāna or 'little way' (the ethico-psychological), the Mahāyāna or 'great way' (the metaphysical-devotional), and the Vajrayāna or 'adamantine way' (the ritualistic-yogic). From the time of Trisong Detsen the Buddhism of all schools was of this triyāna character.

So although Tibetan Buddhism is described as a branch of the Mahāyāna, this is not really accurate. All its schools follow the Hīnayāna in respect both of monastic discipline and organization, as well as all the basic teachings such as the Four Noble Truths, the Noble Eightfold Path, and the twelve links of Conditioned Co-production. All these teachings in Tibetan Buddhism are derived from the first, or Hīnayāna, phase of Indian Buddhism, especially in its Sarvāstivādin form. As regards philosophy, all Tibetan schools follow the Mahāyāna, especially the two great traditions of Indian Buddhist thought, the Mādhyamika, the teaching of the middle way between extremes, and the Yogācāra, the teaching of yoga (in the sense of meditation). Also from the Mahāyāna comes Tibetan Buddhism's overall spiritual ideal, that of the Bodhisattva. And its ritual and its esoteric meditation are taken from the Vajrayāna or Tantra. In this way, all the schools of Tibetan Buddhism are composite in character.

Furthermore, Tibetan Buddhism regards the three yānas not just as three successive stages in the historical development of Buddhism, but as constituting successive stages of the spiritual path for each individual Buddhist. This idea is especially associated with Atīśa, who went from India to Tibet and taught there in the eleventh century. Though a late development in Indian Buddhism, it plays a prominent part in the structure of all schools of Tibetan Buddhism.

Hence we cannot distinguish schools of Tibetan Buddhism as being either Tantric or non-Tantric, as some early Western writers on Tibetan Buddhism tried to do. All schools accept this threefold structure both in terms of the historical development of Buddhism and within the spiritual life of the individual. All accept all three yānas, and all regard the Tantra as the highest flowering, the culmination, of Buddhism. In the West the Tantra has been widely misunderstood and is often thought rather shocking. But for Tibetan Buddhists the Tantra represents the highest and most sacred stage in the development of Buddhism.

The second characteristic common to all Tibetan Buddhist schools is that they accept the same scriptures as their canonical basis – though, as we shall see, the Nyingmapas have certain extra texts. These scriptures comprise the Kangyur, which is in 100, or in some editions 108, xylograph volumes, and the Tangyur, which is in 225 volumes. The Kangyur comprises translations into Tibetan of the sūtras and tantras, in other words all those works which are traditionally believed to be the utterance of the Buddha himself or of one of his Enlightened disciples speaking under his inspiration and guidance. These include texts such as the Perfection of Wisdom literature, the *Saddharma-puṇḍarīka*, and the *Laṅkāvatāra*, in Tibetan translation. The Tangyur consists of translations of commentaries and other expository works by the great Indian Buddhist sages and philosophers – Nāgārjuna, Dharmakīrti, Dignāga, and others.

A volume of one of these texts consists, like all Tibetan books, of oblong pages of tough hand-made paper, usually made from bamboo and very thick and crisp; they make quite a sound as you turn them over. The pages are stacked between wooden covers, not bound together but loose, and you just turn them over one by one as you read them. They are quite massive, so that to speak of a 'small Tibetan library' would be something of a contradiction in terms. Usually libraries contain hundreds of these enormous and heavy volumes. Once when I was studying a Tibetan painting of the Wheel of Life, I noticed that the sphere which we would call hell – that is, the realm of torment and punishment – showed people being crushed by these enormous volumes of the sacred texts. (When I asked a Tibetan friend what this meant, he said that these were people who had not shown respect for the scriptures.)

The third common characteristic of all schools is that those of their followers who happen to be monks all follow the same vinaya, the same pattern of monastic life and observance. Thus the four schools have a lot in common; in fact, the similarities are greater than the differences. Nevertheless differences do exist, each school having distinctive features which are of great significance.

THE NYINGMA SCHOOL

The name Nyingma means 'Old School', and it is so called because it follows the old translations of the tantras, those which were made before the time of King Ralpachen. It's rather as though there were in this country a Christian church which insisted on following only the Authorized Version of the Bible, ignoring the Revised Version and other modern translations.

The Nyingmapas regard the great Indian teacher Padmasambhava, the Lotus-born One, as their founder, and such is their respect for him and devotion to him that they sometimes refer to him as the second Buddha. According to the Nyingma tradition, Padmasambhava has eight principal forms in which he manifests in eight different regions of the world, and Śākyamuni, the historical Buddha, is regarded as being simply one of these.

You can see this emphasis in Nyingma temples. These are usually three-storied. As you enter, you find on the ground floor an enormous image, usually many times larger than life, of the great guru Padmasambhava. He is dressed in royal robes with the lotus cap, seated with the *khatvanga* in the crook of his arm, a skull cup containing blood or nectar in one hand, and a *vajra* or diamond-thunderbolt in the other, and with his characteristic 'wrathfully smiling' expression. Usually images of his two consorts, the Indian princess Mandāravā and the Tibetan yoginī Yeshe Tsogyal, are placed on either side of him. All around there are different frescoes and images, and you generally find Gautama the

Buddha in a corner somewhere, a very minor figure in this pantheon. For the Nyingmapas, Padmasambhava is everything. He has become the embodiment of the ideal of Buddhahood, more so than even Śākyamuni himself.

By all the accounts that have come down to us, Padmasambhava was a many-sided character. He was a brilliant scholar and dialectician, and often worsted the Brahmin scholars in debate. He was a respected sage and teacher, a prolific author, and also a renowned yogi and ascetic, spending much of his time in meditation. Furthermore he was a magician. According to legend he could perform all sorts of wonderful feats. He was, it would seem, one of the greatest masters of the occult that the world has ever seen. And according to some accounts he was also an accomplished dancer. In Tibet he is always referred to as Guru Rimpoche, which means 'the greatly precious teacher', rather than as Padmasambhava, it being considered disrespectful to use someone's personal name.

The Nyingma tradition reflects the many-sidedness of its legendary founder, and in my own opinion, after considerable contact with this school, I would say that it is the richest form of Tibetan Buddhism. It is therefore very difficult to generalize about it. Nyingma teaching of course accepts the triyāna framework, but it is a distinctive feature of this tradition that it subdivides the three yānas into nine, a division which is the basis of that system of practice.

First in this enumeration is the *śrāvakayāna*, the path of the disciple. *Śrāvaka* or disciple here means someone who does not find out the Truth by himself but hears it from an Enlightened teacher, a Buddha, and then directs his efforts towards his own individual emancipation. So while he (or she) makes a genuine effort to attain liberation from saṁsāra, that effort is made solely for his own benefit, no thought being given to the spiritual welfare of others.

Secondly there is the yāna of the *pratyekabuddha*. *Pratyeka* means private or solitary, so the *pratyekabuddha* is one who finds out the Truth by his own efforts. He has no teacher, but also no disciples because he does not care to pass on what he has discovered, being concerned only with his own spiritual emancipation. The *pratyekabuddha*, like the *śrāvaka*, is a kind of spiritual individualist.

The third yāna is the *bodhisattvayāna*. The Bodhisattva has a teacher and also aspires to have disciples, because the aim of the Bodhisattva is to gain Enlightenment not just for his or her own sake but for the benefit of all living beings. He makes the effort to develop spiritually so that he can help and guide other beings; and he does this by practising the six (or ten) *pāramitās* or perfect virtues. Thus the bodhisattvayāna is the path of unmitigated spiritual altruism.

Fourthly there is the *kriyāyoga tantrayāna*. *Kriyā* literally means 'ritual', and this yāna involves a certain amount of external symbolical ritual together with repetition of the mantra and visualization of a particular Buddha (this is described in more detail in Chapter 7). Fifthly there is the *ubhayayoga tantrayāna*. *Ubhaya* means 'both sides' or 'equally', so this is the yāna in which ritual and meditation are practised equally. The sixth yāna is called the *yoga tantrayāna* and comprises various practices for developing the union of Wisdom and Compassion, so that neither exceeds the other. These second three yānas are collectively called the 'Exoteric Tantra' or the *mantrayāna*.

The last three yānas of the Nyingmapas' ninefold scheme comprise the Vajrayāna proper, the Esoteric or 'Inner' Tantra. The seventh is the *mahāyogayāna*, consisting mainly of the practices known as the 'growing' yoga and the 'perfect' yoga (which will be explained later). The eighth is the *anuyogayāna*, which comprises all meditation exercises connected with the control of the breath, the nervous system and psychic centres, and sexual energy. Its aim is the sublimation of all the different gross and subtle forces of the personality of the individual in the direction of Enlightenment. Ninthly there is the *atiyogayāna*. This is the direct practice and realization of the highest truth without any intermediaries at all, and corresponds very roughly to Ch'an or Zen in the fullest sense. There are several different traditions of *atiyogayāna* practice, the most important being *dzogchen* or the 'Great Perfection'. The Nyingmapas maintain special monasteries for this practice.

The way in which the three yānas are divided into nine is very significant. The first two yānas are seen as Hīnayāna, the third comprises the Mahāyāna, and the remaining six cover the Vajrayāna. This reflects the emphasis of the Nyingma School which, while it accepts the triyāna, in practice depends almost entirely on the Vajrayāna or Tantra. Generalizing broadly, when you get a Tantric initiation in the Nyingma tradition, they start off by giving you the three Refuges and the five Precepts, and this represents your practice of the Hīnayāna. Next you take the Bodhisattva vow, which represents your practice of the Mahāyāna. All this usually only takes a few minutes, and then the rest of the initiation is concerned entirely with the Vajrayāna. The whole emphasis of Nyingma practice is on the Vajrayāna; the Hīnayāna and Mahāyāna are studied and practised to a much lesser degree.

The Nyingmapas accept the same scriptures as the other schools, the Kangyur and the Tangyur, but they also have a collection of what they call the Nyingma tantras. These consist of about 300 Tantric texts which the other schools regard as uncanonical, as not really given out by the Buddha. Western scholars used to think that these were forgeries, that they had been written by Tibetans, and that there were no Sanskrit originals as alleged. But Sanskrit originals of some of the Nyingma tantras have been discovered quite recently in Nepal, so it would seem that at least some of them are genuinely canonical.

The Nyingmapas also have a collection of sixty-four volumes of texts known as the *rinchen terma*, which they consider extremely important. These are the so-called 'concealed scriptures' – *rinchen* meaning a 'great treasure', and *terma* 'what is taken out'. According to legend they were written by Padmasambhava during his visit to Tibet. But then – so the legend goes – he realized that the Tibetans were not ready for these particular teachings, so he hid them in different spots, in caves and under stones, and they are supposed to have been discovered gradually over the centuries. Not surprisingly, Western scholars tend to regard these texts as being simply forgeries. However, the *rinchen terma* contains some very important material which we cannot so easily dismiss. For instance, one of these taken-out texts is the *Bardo Thödol* or *Tibetan Book of the Dead*, a very sublime and important document indeed. It is certainly not the work of an ordinary forger. The author of it would have to have been a very great spiritual teacher, whether Padmasambhava himself or not.

During my stay in Kalimpong I knew many followers of the Nyingma School, including great lamas, ordinary monks, and lay people. They used to come to my own monastery, and we would co-operate over Buddhist meetings and celebrations. In this way I got to know many of them quite well. And I observed that they all placed a very definite emphasis on the practice of meditation, in a way that the Gelugpas didn't. The Gelugpas are very devoted to debate. A couple of monks will get together and, surrounded by an audience, have a sort of dialectical discussion. This is all rigidly prescribed by tradition. The questions and answers are all out of their books of logic and philosophy, and are accompanied by appropriate dramatic gestures. They spend hours or even days practising these debates, and are examined for their proficiency. But the Nyingmapas – with whom the Gelugpas maintain a certain friendly rivalry – profess to regard all this as rather childish, and say that one should spend more time in meditation.

I also noticed that Nyingma lamas tended to be very spontaneous. If you ask a Gelug lama a question, nine times out of ten he will refer you to the appropriate page in Tsongkhapa's writings. He will tend to answer by the book, to stick to tradition rather strictly. The Nyingmapas are also very learned, though without pedantry, but if you ask *them* a question they are likely to answer directly, out of their own experience. Some of the Nyingma lamas I knew were entirely guided by what came to them in their meditation. If they were meditating in the morning and it came to them that they should go and see someone, or hold a big puja – well, as soon as they came out of their meditation they would do it. They were guided by their inner inspiration and tended to speak and act out of this inspiration – something the Gelugpas might have regarded as being rather presumptuous.

One of my own Nyingma teachers, Kachu Rimpoche, was staying with me once in Kalimpong. One morning at breakfast he said to me, 'What do you think I saw in my meditation this morning? I saw a great banner of victory on the roof of your monastery. We must get one put up.' For the next week we were busy buying cloth of various colours in the bazaar and ordering the necessary wooden base from a carpenter, and at the end of the week we were able to hoist the banner of victory up on to the roof. It was six feet high, with flounces of coloured silk surmounted by a golden Dharmachakra. And it was put there simply because the Rimpoche had seen it in his meditation. Subsequently he told me that every morning he'd see in his meditation who would be coming to see him later that day.

He was a remarkable person. Another story about him was told to me by a Buddhist nun, a Frenchwoman who lived in Kalimpong. She had had a number of teachers, and tended to go from one to another, always dissatisfied because they didn't teach her enough or not quickly enough. She was a bit of a handful, to put it mildly. She had a doctorate in philosophy from the Sorbonne and was rather intellectual and difficult to please. On one occasion she had just finished with her latest teacher, and was wandering in the wilds of Sikkim, where she happened to meet Kachu Rimpoche. She was on the look-out for a new teacher, so she entered very eagerly into conversation. She told him what meditation practice she had been doing, and when he asked her how often she had been doing it, she said, 'Oh, every day.' Then he said 'You are not speaking the truth – you haven't done it for six months.' She told me that when he said this she almost jumped out of her skin, because it was true.

Being annoyed with her previous teacher, she had not done that meditation for six months.

Of course, she asked to become Kachu Rimpoche's disciple on the spot – though eventually she became disgruntled with him as well, having found him sprinkling all the sacred images in the shrine-room of Pemayangse Monastery with whisky. There is of course nothing wrong with this. The Nyingmapas have occasion in their rituals to use liquor in a skull-cup, or in a little silver dish; it represents *amṛta* or immortality, and in the course of the ritual they take a single drop in the palm of the hand and drink it. But to her this was all wrong, so off she went. But for a time she was very taken by Kachu Rimpoche.

On another occasion, Kachu Rimpoche and I were having lunch with an American couple who had come to study the mysteries of Tibetan Buddhism in Kalimpong. At one point the young man said to me laughingly, 'You know the old story about people levitating. Ask the lama if he has ever seen anyone do it.' He meant this as a joke, but the lama replied very seriously, 'Oh yes, I've seen people do this in Tibet; in fact I can do it a little myself.' When he heard this, the young American almost fell off his chair. In the course of the conversation with this young couple, I noticed that Kachu Rimpoche at times answered their questions before I had had time to translate, even though some of the questions were quite complex. Later on, I questioned him a little more closely on the subject of levitation, and he told me that he couldn't just levitate on the spot. He had to isolate himself for about six months in a secluded cave or jungle somewhere in order to develop the requisite state of mind.

These stories illustrate the nature of the Nyingma lama and the general nature of the Nyingma tradition. The Nyingmapas are often more spontaneous and lively than other lamas. They are also much less organized, especially compared to the Gelugpas. Traditionally the Gelugpas have tended to think in terms of enormous monasteries in Lhasa from which directives would go flying to all the subordinate monasteries. The Nyingmapas tended to be much more on their own, with individual lamas having their own circles of monk and lay disciples. They are also less exclusively monastic. Some of the greatest Nyingma lamas are not monks at all. Another of my own teachers, Dudjom Rimpoche, one of the most famous Nyingma lamas, was a layman with a family.

THE KAGYU SCHOOL

Ka means simply 'speech', and *gyu* is 'tradition', so the name means the school of the oral tradition or oral lineage. The Kagyupas place very little emphasis on scriptural study. They attach much more importance to what they call 'ear-whispered instructions', instructions which the guru gives directly to the disciple and which may in fact never have been written down. The Kagyu School traces its lineage back to the eleventh century, to the great Indian – or rather Bhutanese – teacher Marpa, who had studied in India under Naropa.

The most famous figure of this school is Milarepa. His name means simply 'Mila who wears cotton cloth', and he is surely one of the most vivid and interesting characters in the history of Buddhism, indeed in the whole history of religion. Apparently his father died when he was quite small, and his aunt and uncle robbed him and his widowed mother of their inheritance so that they were left penniless. Milarepa's mother wanted revenge, and encouraged her son to learn black magic. He studied and practised sorcery for many years, and eventually wreaked a terrible vengeance on his relations. But afterwards he was overcome with remorse, because many lives had been lost as a result of his practices.

Eventually he came to the feet of the great guru Marpa, who saw at once that Milarepa was an immensely gifted person, a spiritual genius. But he also saw that he had done a great deal of harm and had to be purified. Marpa was nothing if not a spiritual disciplinarian, and he put Milarepa through such difficult trials that Milarepa was reduced to despair and even wanted to commit suicide. But he was encouraged and helped by Marpa's wife (apparently without her husband's knowledge) and eventually, after many struggles, he was initiated and sent to meditate in the solitude of the high mountains.

If we look at the life of Milarepa thereafter – he lived to be quite an old man – its most prominent feature is his sheer uncompromisingness. He never did things by halves, never made concessions, never gave way even by a fraction. For instance there are all sorts of things which a monk is allowed to possess, but Milarepa would have none of them. He did not wear any robes, just his piece of cotton cloth. At one time he had an earthenware bowl in which he used to boil the nettles he gathered for his meal, but one day the bowl broke and then he truly had nothing.

Another story relates how once Milarepa was asleep in his cave. It was a cold winter's night, and he had no clothes. There was no blanket in the cave, no fire, no food: nothing. In the middle of the night he was woken up by the sound of someone moving about in the cave, and realized that it was a robber. Milarepa was quite amused by this, and called out, 'I don't know how you'll find anything by night, I couldn't find anything by day.' Tibetans – even robbers apparently – have a great sense of humour, so the robber laughed and went away.

Milarepa is traditionally said to have been the greatest yogi in Tibet. There was no spiritual practice, no form of meditation, no attainment of which he was not the master. He was also a remarkable teacher, besides being Tibet's greatest poet. The best-known collection of his poetry is the *Mila Grubum*, the 100,000 songs of Milarepa (there are not literally 100,000; in Tibetan the title really means 'the collected songs'). These poems are not only of profound spiritual import, but often quite wonderful as poetry.

The Kagyu School, following in the footsteps of Milarepa, stresses the actual practice of Buddhism much more than study of the theory, and until the Chinese occupation there were many Kagyu hermits living in remote, inaccessible places in Tibet. Kagyu practices consist mainly of the six Dharmas or Yogas of Naropa. The first of these is the generating of psychic or internal heat. It was his mastery of this that enabled Milarepa to live amidst the snow and ice of the high mountain ranges clad in only a single cotton garment. In modern times one finds Kagyu lamas wearing their single piece of cotton cloth – which is *all* they are supposed to wear if they are practising the yoga of psychic heat – over their thick woollen robes. This suggests that things are not quite what they were in Milarepa's day.

The second of the six Dharmas of Naropa is the realizing of the illusory nature of personality, of one's own individual being. The third is the practice of realizing that the whole of existence is like a dream. Fourthly there is the comprehending of the clear light of the Void. The fifth Dharma is gaining Enlightenment in the after-death state, a practice which is connected with the teaching of the *Tibetan Book of the Dead*. And the sixth Dharma or Yoga of Naropa is the transference of consciousness, not just into other forms of life but into higher states of being.

These six Dharmas involve many complex yogic practices and exercises. However, the highest of the Kagyu practices is the *mahāmudra* or 'great symbol', which corresponds to the *atiyoga* or 'supreme yoga' of the Nyingmapas as well as approximating in some ways to Ch'an or Zen in the very highest sense.

THE SAKYA SCHOOL

This term *sakya* has nothing to do with the Indian word *śākya*, the name of the tribe to which the Buddha belonged. In Tibetan, *sakya* means 'tawny earth', in the sense of fallow or unploughed land, and it is the name of the principal monastery of this school, which was situated in a place known as 'the region of tawny earth'. The school was begun in 1073CE by the great teacher Drokmi, who had studied in India for a number of years under many spiritual masters. However, Drokmi's disciple Könchok Gyelpo is usually regarded as the founder of the school, and he was not a monk but a layman. Though the early heads of the school were married, subsequently it became the custom for them to be monks and to be succeeded by a nephew who was also a monk. Thus when the head of the Sakya School dies, his brother's or his sister's son will succeed, and when *he* dies, the succession will revert to *his* nephew. In this way the succession goes backwards and forwards between two collateral family branches.

The Sakyapas are especially distinguished for their scholarship. The greatest of their scholars, perhaps the greatest of all Tibetan scholars, was the celebrated Butön, who lived in the fourteenth century. He it was who was responsible for the compilation of the Kangyur and the Tangyur, and his collection of the Buddhist texts into these two great editions is accepted as standard and authoritative by all schools of Tibetan Buddhism. He also wrote an important history of Buddhism, covering Buddhism in India as well as in Tibet. Another great historian, Tāranātha, belonged to an offshoot of the Sakya tradition.

Historically there is a close connection between the Sakyapas and the Mongols, as it was the Sakyapas who converted this rather warlike people to Buddhism. Out of gratitude for the teaching they had received, the Mongols supported the Sakyapas politically to such an extent that the supreme abbot of the Sakya School ruled practically the whole of Tibet for a period of about eighty years, spanning the second half of the thirteenth century and the first half of the fourteenth. They can thus be said to have paved the way for the later rule of the Dalai Lamas.

In connection with this there is an interesting story about Pakpa, who consolidated the political power of the Sakyapas in Tibet in the thirteenth century. This celebrated Sakya leader was the guru of the even more famous Kublai Khan, who at that time ruled not only China, but also the whole of Central Asia and even parts of the West. Kublai Khan was apparently very grateful for the spiritual instruction and inspiration which Pakpa had given him, and very devoted to the Sakya School. One day he proposed to Pakpa that he should make a law compelling all the people of Tibet to give up the other traditions and follow only the teaching of the Sakya School. Such was Kublai Khan's enthusiasm.

Now one might have expected Pakpa to have been overjoyed at this development. One might have thought that he would have agreed at once with Kublai Khan's proposal and even have urged him to punish those who refused to conform. After all, such has been the pattern of religious history in the West. But Pakpa did not agree. On the contrary, he dissuaded Kublai Khan from making such a law. Such a law, he said, would not be in accordance with the Dharma. In effect Pakpa was saying that the other Buddhists of Tibet, the non-Sakyapas, should be free to follow whatever school they wished. There must be no compulsion, no coercion. This is, in fact, the Buddhist tradition, and it is very much the attitude of Tibetan Buddhists. They are very devoted to their own form of Buddhism; they believe in it, and follow it wholeheartedly. But at the same time they respect other traditions. Rarely is there any attempt to coerce anybody into a particular school. This is indeed the attitude of Buddhists throughout the East. They are generally very tolerant, whether towards other forms of Buddhism or other religions.

THE GELUG SCHOOL

The Gelugpas are, literally, 'the virtuous ones'. Not that the followers of the other schools were not virtuous, but the Gelugpas specialized, as it were, in virtue; it was their strong point. The Gelug School was founded by Tsongkhapa in the fourteenth century, and is the school to which the Dalai Lamas especially belong, as we shall see in Chapter 3.

This fourth and latest of the great schools of Tibetan Buddhism cannot be understood apart from the character and career of its founder Tsongkhapa, who is undoubtedly one of the greatest figures in Tibetan Buddhism. He embodies the characteristic spiritual or religious genius of the Tibetan people. He is known primarily as the reformer of Buddhism in Tibet, as he swept away many abuses. He was also a great organizer; he unified the monastic Sangha to a considerable extent and imposed a consistent discipline. And he is renowned as a scholar-saint of the highest distinction. Saints are often not scholars, and only too often scholars are by no means saints. But Tsongkhapa was that rather rare combination, a man of saintly life and at the same time a scholar, and both almost to perfection.

Tsongkhapa's life is very well documented, the Tibetans having always been very historically-minded. Here they differ from the ancient Indians. Sanskrit literature is one of the richest in the world, including drama, poetry, and fiction, but it can boast just one historical work. The Tibetans, on the other hand, produced many histories of India, of Tibet, and of Buddhism, as well as innumerable biographies, mainly of saints and religious people, which are often sound critical works, not just hagiography. Hence we know that Tsongkhapa was born in the year 1357CE, the fourth son of his parents, and that, like many other famous and illustrious men, he came from a very poor family. He was born in Tsongkha – literally 'onion valley' – in the province of Amdo in north-eastern Tibet; the famous Kumbum Monastery, the monastery of the 100,000 Buddha images, was later built over the place of his birth.

Tsongkhapa therefore means 'the man from the onion valley'. This again reflects the Tibetan notion that it is disrespectful to refer to people by their personal names. For any respectable, especially religious person, they coin some sort of title. This happened to me when I arrived in Kalimpong. Most Tibetans there never knew that my name was Sangharakshita because nobody ever used it. During the first few years they called me Imji Gelong, which means 'the English monk'; and when I had been there a few years they called me Imji Gelong Geshe Rimpoche. Tsongkhapa's monastic name, given to him on his ordination, was Sumatikīrti which is a Sanskrit name meaning one who is praised, or is praiseworthy, on account of superior intelligence – a very appropriate name for Tsongkhapa. The Tibetans also refer to him as Jetsun Tsongkhapa – Jetsun meaning 'the venerable one' – or as Je Rimpoche, which means 'the greatly precious ruler', the spiritual sovereign as it were.

He seems to have been precocious, not to say a prodigy; his religious education began at the age of three, when he received various initiations and started practising meditation, and he became a śrāmaṇera, a novice monk, at the age of seven. According to the Vinaya, the Book of the Discipline, you can be ordained if you are old enough to earn your living by scaring crows away from the crops (a very important occupation in an agricultural country), and in the East this is usually understood to be when you are about seven. So Tsongkhapa was ordained at the earliest possible opportunity; this is not unusual even today in Buddhist countries. Indeed, there are records in the Buddhist scriptures of little boys of seven, eight, and nine attaining arhantship or Enlightenment. This only goes to show what one can do and how far one can get if one only starts early enough, before one has been corrupted by what Thomas Traherne, the seventeenth century English poet and mystic, calls 'the dirty devices of this world'.

At sixteen Tsongkhapa was sent to study at a number of famous monasteries in central Tibet. For a number of years he moved from one great teacher to another, in this way systematically covering the whole field of Buddhist studies. He studied the voluminous Tibetan scriptures and also the translations of works by the great Indian Buddhist sages and philosophers, which are even more voluminous. In particular he studied logic – in later life he was very strong on logic – as well as mathematics and the Indo-Tibetan ayurvedic tradition of medical science. In addition to this, of course, he studied and practised the teachings of all three yānas of Buddhism.

Thus in his own teaching work, Tsongkhapa had a rich source of material to draw upon. By his time Buddhism had been firmly established in Tibet for several hundred years, and practically everything of importance had been translated and could be studied. Tsongkhapa was therefore able to take quite an encyclopaedic approach. He immersed himself in all the existing traditions, took the best of them, and codified and systematized these in a manner which is still of the utmost importance for the study of Tibetan Buddhism.

At the age of twenty-five he received his full ordination as a Buddhist monk. This 'higher ordination', as it is also called, is available to monks at twenty, but as he was busy with his studies he deferred it until he was twenty-five. After that he was fully occupied both with continuing his studies and with teaching; and the remaining thirty or so years of his life were passed in this way. In the course of these years he gathered many disciples who, on account of their devotion and dedication to the Dharma and the purity and holiness of their lives, gradually became known as the Gelugpas, meaning 'the virtuous ones'. They were so called because, following Tsongkhapa's example, they insisted on a stricter observance of the vinaya than was customary at that time, including a total prohibition of marriage and of alcohol.

In the West the Gelugpas are often known as the Yellow Hats, in contradistinction to members of the older schools who are known as the Red Hats and to some of the Kagyu off-shoots who are called the White Hats or Black Hats. This distinction relates to certain Tantric ceremonies, at least with regard to the Yellow Hats and the Red Hats. At the time of Tantric initiation, the officiating lama or guru puts on a cap – yellow in the case of the Gelugpas, red in the case of the Nyingmapas – and this has a definite significance. The cap is put on at those moments in the ceremony when the lama is identifying himself mentally, through meditation, with the Buddha or Bodhisattva whose initiation he is giving.

So when an acolyte hands the yellow cap – or the red cap, as the case may be – to the guru, this is a very solemn moment. The cap is usually handed over ceremoniously on a piece of silk or a cushion. When the guru puts it on, you know that he is at that moment identifying himself in his meditation with the Buddha or Bodhisattva whose initiation he is about to give. The recipient of the initiation therefore feels that he is receiving it from the Buddha or Bodhisattva himself, through the guru. After that moment has passed, the hat is solemnly taken off and given back to the acolyte, to be folded up and put away. Up to the time of Tsongkhapa all the lamas, following the Indian tradition, used to have red caps for this purpose. Tsongkhapa wanted to make a visible distinction between his followers and those of the existing schools, so he changed the colour of the hat used in these ceremonies from red to yellow.

In the course of Tsongkhapa's lifetime his disciples founded in or near Lhasa, the capital of Tibet, three great Gelug monasteries: Ganden, Sera, and Drepung. These have survived to the present day, although they have been seriously damaged by the Chinese. Before the Chinese occupation Ganden and Sera each housed about 5,000 monks, and Drepung was even bigger, with over 7,000. They were almost like monastic towns or even cities.

Tsongkhapa was a prolific author; the standard collected edition of his writings fills sixteen massive Tibetan volumes. His two principal works are the *Lam-rim chen-mo* and the *Ngak-rim chen-mo*. *Lam-rim* literally means 'stages of the path' (*chen-mo* means 'great'); the work is a survey of the whole spiritual path according to the Mahāyāna tradition, discussing in detail the practice of the *pāramitās* and so on, citing innumerable Buddhist scriptures. The Nga-rim is a similar account of the Tantric Path, that is, the Vajrayāna. These two comprehensive and highly systematic works are the basis of Gelug studies. Tsongkhapa also wrote a shortened version of the Lam-rim for those of lesser intelligence, and this is the one which even the monks usually study, the longer version being extremely difficult, abstruse, and technical. Besides these, he composed some commentaries on scriptures, and a number of rather beautiful minor works.

Tsongkhapa died in the year 1419, by which time the Gelug Order and the movement which it represented was well established, with a firm footing in the religious life of Tibet. Thereafter the anniversary of his death was observed every year – not just by the Gelugpas but by all schools – with a great festival of lights. As the evening draws in and it begins to get dark, people put rows of tiny oil or butter lamps round every house, monastery, and temple, in the windows, along the parapets, on the flat roofs, on the window sills. Hundreds or even thousands of these lamps can be seen all over the town, presenting a beautiful sight.

On account of the force of his personality, his vast scholarship and organizational ability, and his spiritual genius, Tsongkhapa left a permanent imprint on Tibetan Buddhism. But even more than this, in the estimation of the Tibetan people, especially the Gelugpas, Tsongkhapa is above all a Bodhisattva. He is traditionally regarded as a manifestation of the Bodhisattva Manjuśrī, the Bodhisattva of Wisdom, who is associated in particular with the Perfection of Wisdom teachings. Tibetan paintings or images representing Tsongkhapa therefore show him with the attributes and insignia of Manjuśrī. He is depicted as a rather typical Tibetan scholar-saint, seated in his monastic robes and wearing his tall yellow cap, but growing out of his shoulders, as it were, rather like two little wings, are lotus flowers. On one lotus is the flaming sword of Manjuśrī, the sword which cuts asunder the bonds of ignorance, and on the other is the book of the Perfection of Wisdom scriptures. This indicates that Tsongkhapa is regarded as a manifestation on the earthly plane of Manjuśrī, the great archetype of spiritual wisdom.

ཨོཾ་མ་ཎི་པདྨེ་ཧཱུྃ། ཨོཾ་མ་ཎི་པདྨེ་ཧཱུྃ། ཨོཾ་མ་ཎི་པདྨེ་ཧཱུྃ།

ཨོཾ་མ་ཎི་པདྨེ་ཧཱུྃ། ཨོཾ་མ་ཎི་པདྨེ་ཧཱུྃ། ཨོཾ་མ་ཎི་པདྨེ་ཧཱུྃ།

3

The 'Reincarnations' of the Dalai Lama

Even if they know nothing else about Buddhism, people in the West have all heard of the Dalai Lama. His role and significance, however, are often greatly misunderstood. In fact, this misunderstanding prevails not just in Western countries. I remember when the Chinese first invaded Tibet, and again at the time of the Lhasa uprising in 1959, the newspapers in India, where I was then living, contained all sorts of rather grotesque references to the Dalai Lama which showed quite clearly that they had no idea of his status or function. Some reporters, for instance, would describe him as 'the living Buddha', which of course he is not. Other headlines said something like 'Priest-king flees to India'. Some newspapers went so far as to refer to the Dalai Lama as the Buddhist Pope, the Potala as the Buddhist Vatican, and the leading incarnate lamas as the Buddhist princes of the Church, thus showing that they really did not have the faintest idea of who or what the Dalai Lama really is.

We cannot understand the Dalai Lama, his nature and functions, apart from the general background of Tibetan Buddhism, and especially the background of the Gelug School. This is the school with which he is personally affiliated, though he is revered by Tibetans of all schools.

The Gelugpas continued to flourish after Tsongkhapa's death. Skipping a generation or two, we find that the third abbot of Ganden (one of the three monasteries founded in the Jetsun's lifetime) was a nephew of Tsongkhapa called Gendun Drup. He founded the famous monastery of Tashilhunpo in Shigatse, and installed his own personal teacher as its abbot. Gendun Drup was popularly regarded as the reincarnation of the second abbot of Ganden (Tsongkhapa himself being regarded as Ganden's first abbot), and it is from this time that the idea of what scholars – using a Mongolian term – call Hubalganic succession, that is to say succession by reincarnation, originates.

At this early stage, there were only two lines of Hubalganic succession within the Gelugpa: firstly, the line of successive reincarnations of Tsongkhapa's nephew, the third abbot of Ganden; and secondly, those of his teacher, the first abbot of Tashilhunpo. These two lines subsequently became known as those of the Dalai Lama and the Panchen Lama respectively. The Dalai Lamas are the descendants – in the sense of continued reincarnations – of the third abbot of Ganden, whereas the Panchen Lamas are the reincarnations of the first abbot of Tashilhunpo. The present Dalai Lama is the fourteenth of his line of Hubalganic succession, and the late Panchen Lama was the tenth of his particular line.

Though this Hubalganic succession is peculiar to Tibetan Buddhism, it does not represent anything radically new in Buddhism. It is simply a new application of an old principle, one that permeates practically all aspects and schools of Buddhism: the principle of the Bodhisattva ideal. The Bodhisattva ideal, a Mahāyāna conception, embodies the Buddhist spiritual ideal in its loftiest form. It is the ideal of Enlightenment not just for one's own sake but for the benefit of all – the ideal not of individual, but, in a sense, of 'collective' or even cosmic salvation.

Although the Bodhisattva ideal is open to a number of abstruse, metaphysical constructions, it can also be expressed in comparatively simple terms. It needs to be understood in the context of the Buddhist view of karma and rebirth – the idea that people do not live just once on this earth but undergo a succession of lives according to the law of karma, the law of cause and effect working on the psychological and ethical plane. Rebirth, according to Buddhist teaching, takes place on account of the residue of craving, aversion, and ignorance in the individual stream of consciousness (popularly known as the 'soul') at the time of death. In other words, if you have died with your passions unexhausted, if there is something for which you still crave, something to which you are still attached – whether family, or riches, or fame, or even study, even Buddhism itself, perhaps – then you will have to come back. You will be drawn back by the power of your craving, by the power of your desire, your attachment, into a new body, a 'reincarnation'.

This process is depicted by the Tibetan Wheel of Life. In the hub there are three animals – a cock, a snake, and a pig – representing the three mental poisons of craving, aversion, and ignorance which set the whole process going. In the second circle are the upward and the downward paths of ethical and unethical conduct. The third circle shows the six spheres of conditioned existence (including the human realm) into which one can be reborn. The outermost circle consists of the twelve links of the chain of Conditioned Co-production in accordance with which the whole process takes place. This is standard Buddhist teaching. The wheel of birth and death and rebirth revolves on account of the three poisons of craving, aversion, and ignorance.

However, in the course of spiritual practice, one is able gradually to eliminate these three poisons. Craving and aversion become less pronounced, ignorance is dispelled, and in the end there is in one's mind or consciousness only a state of peace, of love, of wisdom. One is no longer bound to the wheel, one no longer has to be reborn. So at death, when the consciousness flashes out of the physical body, there is nothing to draw it back. It remains on the higher, transcendental plane of existence, in the state of undisturbed Enlightenment.

But – and this is a very important but – according to the Mahāyāna, at this point two possibilities, two paths, disclose themselves. Having reached this point one can just remain there and allow oneself to simply 'disappear' into nirvāṇa, to vanish from the ken of the world. On the other hand one can turn back. One can decide, quite voluntarily, to be reborn – not because there is any residue of karma left unaccounted for, but out of compassion, in order to continue to help other living beings in the world with the knowledge and spiritual experience one has gained.

This moment of choice is described in the legend of the great Bodhisattva Avalokiteśvara. It is said that originally, many thousands of years ago, he was a great yogi who had, for most of his life, practised meditation in a cave in the Himalayas. Eventually the time came when he found himself on the verge of Enlightenment, the very brink of nirvāṇa. He ascended from one stage of higher consciousness to another, going further and further away from the world, experiencing all sorts of archetypal and paradisal realms, seeing all sorts of glorious forms and figures. At last even these faded away and he came to the shore of a great ocean of light. He could see, he could hear, nothing but this ocean of light, and with the most profound joy he knew that at last he was returning to his source. He was going to 'merge' with Reality itself. With a great sigh of relief, he started to let go, to allow himself to slip into that great ocean.

But at that very moment he heard a sound, coming as though from a great distance, from far below. At first he did not know what it was, but it arrested his attention and he listened. He became aware of not just one sound but many sounds, many voices, and they were all crying out, wailing, weeping, lamenting, grieving. As he listened the sound became louder and louder until at last he turned away from the great ocean of light, and looked down (hence his name, Avalokiteśvara, which means 'the Lord who looks down'). He looked down into the depths, right down to this world itself, and he saw so many people, so many millions of living beings, suffering in various ways due to their ignorance and their lack of spiritual instruction. And the thought came to him: 'How can I leave these beings? How can I allow myself to merge into this ocean of light, just saving myself, when there are in the world below so many beings who need my help and assistance and guidance?' So he turned back. He not only looked down; he went down, he went back into the world.

The first path, that of allowing oneself to merge into nirvāṇa, is considered – at least by the Mahāyāna – to be the path of the arhant, the one who desires individual salvation. The second path, that chosen by Avalokiteśvara, is the path of the Bodhisattva, the one who desires not just his (or her) own emancipation but also the liberation and Enlightenment of all living beings whatsoever, and who is not satisfied until he can gather them all into his arms and carry them to Buddhahood, to a sort of cosmic Enlightenment. The path of the Bodhisattva is traditionally regarded as a separate and higher path from that of the arhant. However, in a sense the path of the Bodhisattva includes and contains that of the arhant, inasmuch as one must have the capacity to gain liberation for oneself if one's renunciation of that individual liberation is to have any significance. Otherwise the Bodhisattva path may be not so much a spiritual ideal as a mere rationalization of one's attachment to the world.

Tibetan Buddhists take the Bodhisattva ideal very seriously. For them it is a real, living thing. Marco Pallis called it 'the presiding idea of Tibetan Buddhism', and if we do not understand it we have probably not understood Tibetan Buddhism. The Tibetans believe that there are people, currently living in the world, who have made this great sacrifice, people who have literally turned their backs upon nirvāṇa and returned to the world to help in the higher evolution of the human race towards Enlightenment. For Tibetans the Bodhisattva ideal is not just a beautiful myth, it is not – as I have found it described by a Roman Catholic writer – just a spiritual pipe-dream (in contrast, the implication being, to the historical reality of the crucified Christ). Tibetans regard the Bodhisattvas as being very much with us, as being part of what we might call the 'spiritual economy' of the world; and they believe very strongly that some of these Bodhisattvas can be identified. And the Bodhisattvas they identify include the Dalai Lamas and the Panchen Lamas.

The Dalai Lama is regarded as a manifestation of Avalokiteśvara, the Bodhisattva of Compassion, while the Panchen Lama is believed to be a manifestation of Amitābha, the Buddha of Infinite Light. But if one is supposed to be a Buddha and the other a Bodhisattva, what sort of distinction (one might wonder) is being made here? In this context, the difference between a Buddha and a Bodhisattva is the distinction between the static and the dynamic aspects of the same spiritual reality. The Buddha represents the static aspect of Enlightenment, not in the sense of standing still *in* time but standing outside time altogether. The Bodhisattva represents that same eternal transcendental experience in its dynamic aspect, in other words, in the process of realization within historical time.

Technically a Buddha could be seen as superior to a Bodhisattva, for which reason some Western scholars have assumed that the Panchen Lama must occupy a higher position than the Dalai Lama, that the Dalai Lama may be the temporal ruler of Tibet, but the Panchen Lama must be the spiritual head. This sounds logical, but it is not the case. In the eyes of the Tibetans, the Dalai Lama is all in all – he is the temporal ruler, *de jure* if not *de facto*, and he is also the spiritual head of Tibet. The Panchen Lama is in comparison a rather shadowy figure.

Tibetans in Kalimpong always had on their shrines a large framed photograph of the Dalai Lama; very rarely would there be one of the Panchen Lama. So when in the winter of 1956 the Dalai Lama and the Panchen Lama were officially welcomed at Siliguri airport and (through the machinations of the Chinese, who were semi-sponsoring the Panchen Lama) the two of them were provided with thrones of the same height, the Tibetans were highly indignant.

From their earliest years the Dalai Lamas are given a very careful training in all departments of Buddhist thought and Buddhist life. They learn to meditate and they undertake a difficult course of study and practice. So by the time a Dalai Lama reaches his majority he is usually very well-informed about all aspects of Buddhist tradition, both theoretical and practical. At the same time, despite his great learning, despite his immense authority and prestige, the Dalai Lama is never regarded as any kind of supreme doctrinal authority. He is not responsible for laying down how Tibetan Buddhists should practise Buddhism, nor even how Gelug Buddhists should practise. If anyone has this function it is a comparatively subordinate figure, the Ti Rimpoche, who is the abbot of the Ganden Monastery. Thus the Dalai Lama's position in Tibetan Buddhism is in no way analogous to that of the Pope in the Roman Catholic Church. The Pope defines morals and dogma, but the Dalai Lama does no such thing.

The third, fifth, and thirteenth Dalai Lamas are of special historical importance. The third Dalai Lama lived in the sixteenth century, roughly contemporary with England's Queen Elizabeth I, and it was he who finally converted the Mongols. They had originally been converted – as we saw in the previous chapter – by Pakpa, the Sakya hierarch, but subsequently fell away from Buddhism after the collapse of their empire in China. The third Dalai Lama was responsible for bringing them back into the fold of Buddhism, and thereafter they became staunch followers of the Gelug School. Indeed, learned as the Gelugpas are, the Mongolians came to surpass them in learning. They are formidable scholars. I once travelled with a Mongolian lama, and whenever we stopped, out would come a book. He'd put a silk cloth across his knees, open the book, and start studying. Day and night he never did anything else. He was indefatigable.

It was the third Dalai Lama who first received the title of Dalai Lama from Altan Khan, the ruler of the Mongols, and it was then bestowed posthumously on his predecessors. The word *dalai* is Mongolian, and means 'great like the ocean', so *dalai lama* means 'the lama, or teacher, who is great like the ocean'. This is the title used when they are speaking to Westerners, but amongst themselves Tibetans usually refer to the Dalai Lama either as *galwa rimpoche*, which means 'precious ruler', or *yeshe norbu*, which means 'jewel of knowledge'.

The fifth Dalai Lama, known as the 'Great Fifth', lived in the seventeenth century. He was a very learned man, a great scholar and author. Although he was the leading representative of the Gelug School, he was very sympathetic to the Nyingma School and wrote several books on the Nyingma tradition. In addition to writing a great deal on purely religious subjects, he wrote on history, grammar, poetry, and astrology. He was a great statesman and administrator, and with the support of the Mongols he took over the temporal rule of Tibet. He also started building the Potala, the famous seat of the Dalai Lamas in Lhasa, named after Avalokiteśvara's legendary abode in South India.

So it is from the days of the Great Fifth that Tibet became what we in the West call a theocracy, a sort of religious state. We tend to think of the Dalai Lamas and the theocracy of Tibet as something fixed and established for all time, as being typically Tibetan, but in fact it is a comparatively recent development. Tibet has been a theocracy for only 300 out of the 1,300 years of Tibetan Buddhist history.

The thirteenth Dalai Lama ruled in the present century, and it was he who reasserted Tibet's independence from China after the collapse of the Manchu dynasty. He also tightened up the training of monks. When on the occasion of the Younghusband expedition to Lhasa the thirteenth Dalai Lama took refuge in Mongolia, in the course of his discussions with Mongolian lamas he found, rather to his consternation (so Dhardo Rimpoche, one of my Tibetan teachers, told me), that they were referring to texts which he had never studied. On his return to Lhasa he therefore reorganized the curriculum of studies for monks.

As for the present Dalai Lama, he was discovered and identified in 1935. Having fled from Tibet after the Lhasa uprising of 1959, he now lives in exile in Dharamsala in northern India. There have been prophecies to the effect that he will be the last of the line, and many Tibetans believe this. However, nobody can say with any certainty what the future holds.

The tragic story of Tibet in recent years has highlighted what the Dalai Lama means to the Tibetans. To begin with, he is regarded as the temporal ruler of the Tibetan people, and as such he is the focal point of the national consciousness. Both for Tibetans in Tibet who do not accept the Chinese rule, and for those in exile in India and elsewhere, he is the symbol, even the incarnation, of the Tibetan national spirit. But his significance is by no means confined to that.

Above all, the Dalai Lama is for the Tibetans a Bodhisattva living in their midst. Whatever *we* might think, the Tibetans take this quite literally, just as the pious Catholic regards the Pope as infallible. The Dalai Lama is not just a very good man, not just the ruler of the country, not just an eminent teacher or a great spiritual figure. He is for the Tibetans quite literally Avalokiteśvara, manifest in the world. They feel that through him the whole of Tibet, the whole of their tradition, the whole of their life, is in contact with the archetypal world, in contact with the transcendental. This is why he is the focal point of so much spiritual emotion, so much devotion. I have met hundreds if not thousands of Tibetans of all shades of opinion, all social classes, all degrees of education, but there was never any doubt about their absolute devotion to the person of the

Dalai Lama – a devotion based on the firm belief that he was quite literally a Bodhisattva, one who had earned the freedom of nirvāṇa but who had voluntarily elected to remain behind in the world to help them.

ཨོཾ་མ་ཎི་པདྨེ་ཧཱུྃ། ཨོཾ་མ་ཎི་པདྨེ་ཧཱུྃ། ཨོཾ་མ་ཎི་པདྨེ་ཧཱུྃ།

ཨོཾ་མ་ཎི་པདྨེ་ཧཱུྃ། ཨོཾ་མ་ཎི་པདྨེ་ཧཱུྃ། ཨོཾ་མ་ཎི་པདྨེ་ཧཱུྃ།

4

Monks and Laity in Buddhist Tibet

All Buddhists 'go for refuge' to the 'Three Jewels', the three most precious values for the sake of which everything else in the spiritual life exists. The Three Jewels are the Buddha (the ideal of Enlightenment), the Dharma (his teaching), and the Sangha (the spiritual community of his followers). In this chapter we shall be looking at the third of these 'refuges', the Sangha.

The Sangha exists at three different levels. The *Āryasaṅgha* or 'Noble Sangha' – the spiritual élite, one might say – consists of those who have gained at least a degree of spiritual Insight. They are Enlightened, or well on the way to the goal of Enlightenment. Then there is the Sangha as it exists at the level of formal monastic life, the order of bhikṣus and bhikṣuṇīs – monks and nuns – who have in a sense separated themselves from the world and who devote all their time and energy to the religious life. Thirdly there is the *Mahāsaṅgha,* which includes all those who, whatever their degree of spiritual attainment and regardless of whether they are monks, nuns, or lay people, have committed themselves, at least to some extent, to following the path, practising the Dharma, and realizing the ideal of Buddhahood.

Within the Sangha as it exists – or existed – in Tibet, there are different kinds of monks and teachers, and one may easily get confused about the role and status of each. This chapter describes the various categories of monks and lay followers, how they live and practise, the relations between them, and the great Bodhisattva ideal that inspires and unites them. Much of what pertains to the monks and lay people of Tibet is also true of other Buddhist countries, but Tibetan Buddhism has many unique features and its monks and laity therefore have certain distinctive characteristics.

Tibetan monks belong to the Sarvāstivāda *nikāya* or branch of the Sangha, one of the four *nikāyas* into which the early Indian monastic Sangha split up. At the time of the Buddha's death, the monastic order consisted simply of those of his followers who had given up worldly life to devote themselves to meditation and spiritual practice. There were a number of rules, but on the whole they led a fairly free and easy existence, not unlike that of the modern Hindu sādhu. As time went on the order became more organized, more rules were introduced, and inevitably some differences of opinion occurred. About a hundred years after the Buddha's death the monastic order split into two: the more progressive Mahāsaṅghikas or 'Great Assemblists' and the more conservative Sthaviras, or 'elders'. According to some scholars, the Mahāsaṅghikas may have contributed to the rise of the Mahāyāna.

Over the next two centuries the Sthaviras themselves split, giving rise to the Pudgalavādins or 'Personalists' and the Sarvāstivādins or 'Panrealists'. All four *nikāyas* transmitted essentially the same vinaya, or code of monastic discipline. They eventually subdivided further to make up the eighteen classical schools of early Buddhism which collectively came to be known as the Hīnayāna. Nowadays only two traditions of monastic ordination remain: that of the Sthaviras in their Theravāda form, concentrated in Sri Lanka, Myanmar (Burma), and Thailand; and the Sarvāstivādin lineage, found mainly in Tibet, China, Mongolia, and Vietnam. As we saw in Chapter 1, when King Trisong Detsen in the eighth century decided that Tibetan Buddhism should be a triyāna system, he decreed that it should follow the Sarvāstivāda in vinaya, the Mādhyamika and Yogācāra in philosophy, and the Tantra in meditation. Since that time Tibetan monks have followed a Tibetan translation of the Sarvāstivādin vinaya.

There are six grades of Tibetan monk. The first grade is that of the *genye*. There are two kinds of genye. The first is that of the lay person who observes the five *śīlas* or moral precepts; this corresponds to the Indian *upāsaka* or lay Buddhist. The other kind of genye is a sort of probationer who lives in a monastery, serves the monks, and observes ten ethical precepts. It is this second kind of genye that constitutes the first grade of Tibetan monk.

The second grade is that of the *getsul*, corresponding to the Indian *śrāmaṇera*. A getsul is a novice monk who is studying to become fully ordained and who observes thirty-six precepts. Ordination as a getsul or śrāmaṇera cannot be given before the age of seven or eight (in Tibet reckoned from the inferred date of conception).

Thirdly the *gelong*, the fully ordained monk, corresponds to the Indian *bhikṣu* (Pali *bhikkhu*). One cannot be ordained as a gelong before one's twentieth year, and often one waits until later than this, as did Tsong-khapa who was twenty-five when he took his higher ordination. The Tibetan gelong observes 150 ethical precepts, divided into seven categories, as well as various rules of monastic etiquette. The first category is the most important, containing as it does the four precepts which prohibit sexual intercourse, theft, the deliberate taking of life, and making false claims regarding one's spiritual attainments.

The fourth grade of monk is the *geshe*. This term is sometimes translated as 'doctor of Buddhist divinity' – I even saw this once on the visiting card of an English-speaking Tibetan geshe. But the geshe is better described as the 'learned monk'. There are five chief subjects of study for the geshe, to which he devotes many years of his life. First he studies the vinaya, or monastic discipline. There is a great deal of literature on this subject, some of it rather abstruse. Over the centuries a few simple monastic rules grew into a vast, complex, quasi-legal system; sometimes special 'monk-lawyers' are needed to unravel it before a monk can tell whether or not he has committed an offence.

The geshe's second subject of study is the Abhidharma, a vast body of essentially scholastic Buddhist literature which includes the detailed analysis of mental states into their constituent functions. Thirdly the geshe studies the Prajñāpāramitā or Perfection of Wisdom scriptures, the most important group of Mahāyāna sūtras. Ideally the geshe studies all these sūtras – there are about thirty-five of them plus commentaries. Of these the *Vajracchedikā* or *Diamond Sūtra* is particularly popular in Tibet, and is recited on every possible occasion. The fourth area of study is Mādhyamika philosophy, the teaching of the doctrine of the Middle Way. This highly metaphysical and dialectical tradition, based on the Prajñā-pāramitā scriptures, was founded by the great Indian Buddhist thinker Nāgārjuna early in the Christian era.

Finally the geshe studies logic. Before it was wiped out by Islam, Indian Buddhism had a very rich tradition in this field, and many Indian

Buddhist treatises on logic, by masters such as Dignāga and Dharmakīrti, have been translated into Tibetan. Tibet, and especially the Gelug School, kept up the tradition of the study of logic more than other parts of the Buddhist world, certainly compared to China or Japan where they preferred a more direct, intuitive approach.

Some scholars are of the opinion that the Indian and Tibetan Buddhist logicians eventually got rather far away from the spiritual teachings of the Buddha, but the Tibetans would argue that it is all part of the Bodhisattva ideal. The Bodhisattva aspires to bring everyone on to the path and enable them to mature spiritually, and this is not easy. You have to be able to discuss and debate with people – and how can you do this without rational argument? Logic – along with rhetoric, arts and crafts, and even poetry and dance – is part of the equipment, as it were, by which the Bodhisattva leads all beings on the path to Enlightenment.

It usually takes not less than twelve years, sometimes much longer, to master these five subjects and complete the geshe course. The system of study is largely tutorial, either by individual tuition or in the context of very small classes. Examinations are held yearly, and are entirely oral; there is no written work. On the appointed day the individual candidate comes into the examination hall where, sitting round in a great circle, are hundreds of geshes who have already passed the course. One after another, they fire questions on any of the five subjects. The individual candidate sits in the middle, perhaps quaking a little, and waits for the first question. From the right there will perhaps come a very technical question about the vinaya, which you have to answer at once. No sooner have you answered it than there comes from behind you a question about logic. You answer *that*, and before you have recovered yourself someone asks a question on the Perfection of Wisdom. The questions get more and more difficult; the geshes are trying to catch you out the whole time. The examination goes on for several hours, with questions being fired from all sides.

Even the Dalai Lama has to undergo this gruelling experience. Tibetan friends who were present on the occasion once described to me the current Dalai Lama's geshe examination. Apparently there was one terrible instant when it seemed he was not going to be able to answer the question. But suddenly recovering himself, he came out with the answer with a terrific roar. Everyone was delighted. After all, he *was* the Dalai Lama. He was given a second class pass, which shows the system is quite fair and impartial. (There are four grades of pass, and a first is virtually unheard of.) If you fail the yearly examination, as often happens, you simply carry on studying and try again next time. You can take as long as you like, there being no fixed time limit by which you must complete the course. You present yourself when you feel ready. Obviously, you have to start quite young if you want to get anywhere by middle life.

The whole process of this viva voce examination is strictly stylized: there are certain ritual gestures that have to be observed in the asking and answering of questions. When you put your question you might thrust out your forefinger and fix your opponent with your eye, and if he cannot reply you might make a gesture of triumph. If he can get back at you, he does so with another gesture. It is very animated and dramatic to watch, even if one cannot quite follow the more abstruse exchanges. This type of formalized debate is very popular with the Gelugpas – they spend hours at it. If you go to a monastery you will often find in the courtyard under the trees groups of young monks practising their debating skills. Even when they are engaged in some other business, one of them may suddenly turn to another and fire at him a question about logic, or about the Perfection of Wisdom, so that they are kept on their toes all the time.

The geshe course, although very comprehensive, is concerned only with Hīnayāna and Mahāyāna subjects. The fifth kind of Tibetan monk, however, is one who is proficient in both the theory and the practice of the tantras. This is the *lama gyupa*, which means literally 'the lama in the lineage', that is to say a lama in the guru-disciple tradition of the Tantra. According to the Gelug system, it is only after passing out as a geshe that you go on to take up the full Tantric course. They insist that you should embark upon the study and practice of the Tantra, the Vajrayāna, only after thorough study of the Hīnayāna and the Mahāyāna. The other schools are not so strict and tend to allow people to study the Tantra directly, with little or no acquaintance with the Hīnayāna and Mahāyāna.

The three great monasteries around Lhasa – Ganden, Drepung, and Sera – were used for the geshe course. For Tantric study and practice there were two colleges in Lhasa, which you could join only after having completed the geshe degree. The discipline in these colleges was extremely rigorous. For example, while in the big monasteries you might have your own room, in the colleges you would sleep side by side with only a thin blanket over two or three people. A strict routine was followed, starting very early in the morning – a routine of study, meditation, discussion, and practice of all kinds. My teacher and friend Dhardo Rimpoche joined one of the Tantric colleges after passing out as a geshe from Drepung, but he was only able to remain there for a year because his health broke down under the austere way of life. Apparently this happened quite often.

The lama gyupas, those who have completed the Tantric course, are very highly honoured by both lay people and other monks. When the refugees started pouring out of Tibet, especially after the 1959 Lhasa uprising, there were many monks among them, and I remember that Dhardo Rimpoche was particularly anxious about the fate of the lama gyupas. I asked him why this was, and he explained that what the geshes had studied could be found in books, so that even if the geshes did not survive, the books were available and one could read them. But what the lama gyupas had learned had been transmitted to them orally. The teachings were not recorded in books but in the spiritual experiences of the lama gyupas, and thus were not so easily preserved. If the lama gyupas were not able to pass on the oral traditions to other people, they would be lost for ever.

The sixth grade of Tibetan Buddhist monk is the *khenpo*, a term usually translated as 'abbot'. It corresponds to the Indian *upādhyāya* or 'preceptor', in other words the one who gives ordination. The khenpo is head of the monastery. If the monastery has a number of constituent colleges, as at Drepung and Sera, then each college would have its own abbot, with a sort of grand abbot over them. A khenpo is traditionally appointed by the Dalai Lama on the recommendation of the monastery council. It is a fairly democratic system. When a khenpo dies, the council or governing body of the monastery selects someone from among the geshes and lama gyupas of the monastery – or perhaps from another monastery – to be the new khenpo, and the Dalai Lama confirms this. He very rarely refuses to confirm someone recommended by the council, though he has the power to do so. Under the khenpo there are lay administrators, responsible for the upkeep of the monastery, and various monastic functionaries in charge of things like discipline and ceremonies.

One question remains: where do the incarnate lamas come in? The answer is quite simple. The incarnate lamas, as such, do not come in at all. These six grades of monkhood are achieved either by ordination, or by passing an examination, or by appointment. Incarnate lamas belong to a quite different category. They are not made, they are born. The Dalai Lama, for example, is not elected to that position, and he does not pass an examination to become Dalai Lama. He is not even necessarily the most learned monk. He is simply someone who is recognized as the reincarnation of the previous Dalai Lama. In the same way, all incarnate lamas or *nirmāṇakāyas* – *tulkus*, as the Tibetans call them – are people who are recognized from birth, or from shortly after birth, as being the reincarnations of their predecessors. So the classification of Tibetan monks does not include a separate category of incarnate lama.

Normally, however, especially in the case of the Gelugpas, the incarnate lamas still progress through all six stages. After their discovery or identification, they are ordained as genyes, then when they are seven or eight as getsuls and when they are about twenty as gelongs. Long before that they will have started on their geshe course, often when they are about eight. Starting so early, they also finish early, and sometimes pass out as geshes, with flying colours in some cases, by their mid-twenties. Other monks usually start later and take much longer, but the incarnate lamas seem to go through the process much more quickly. Usually they then become abbot of their predecessor's monastery. And as they are reincarnations of the most distinguished abbots, so they may be regarded as being in a sense a subdivision of the khenpos.

Many Western writers use the word 'lama' indiscriminately to mean a Tibetan monk, but it translates the Sanskrit word *uttama* meaning 'superior', in the sense of the spiritual superior, the teacher, the guru. Tibetan Buddhism places great importance on the figure of the lama. Indeed, it goes so far as to consider the lama as a fourth Jewel of Buddhism. Like Buddhists of all traditions, Tibetan Buddhists recite 'to the Buddha for refuge I go, to the Dharma for refuge I go, to the Sangha for refuge I go,' expressing their commitment to the realization of these three highest values. But before that, Tibetans say 'To the Lama (or Guru) for refuge I go'. They do so because according to the Tibetan tradition you do not even know the Buddha, Dharma, or Sangha except through the lama, the spiritual master or teacher.

Strictly speaking only the lama gyupas and the khenpos are lamas, who may or may not be tulkus. In Tibet, monks are usually referred to collectively as *trapas*, literally 'students', because they go on studying all their lives. Whether they are fifteen or fifty, they have an outlook on life which is very much that of the student, of someone who is interested in study, in knowledge, and is not at all concerned with getting on in the world.

Another term you often hear is *rimpoche*, which is really a mode of address. It translates the Sanskrit *mahāratna*, and means 'great precious one' or 'great jewel'. It is used in speaking to, or about, monks of grades four to six, that is to say, the geshe, the lama gyupa, and the abbot. Incarnate lamas are also addressed as Rimpoche, and occasionally the word is used in addressing very old or very learned and pious monks, even if they are not technically geshes, just to pay respect to their advanced age or great learning.

Monks of all grades nearly always live in *gompas* or monasteries (*gompa* meaning literally 'a place for meditation'). Usually they are registered at a particular monastery, so that they officially belong there and cannot be absent without permission. There are proctors who go round every night making sure every monk is in his cell. They carry great iron-bound staves and bang them on the ground as they go along, to let you know they are coming. You must not be outside the monastery gate after that hour, otherwise you are hauled up in front of the abbot next morning. Monks are allowed to visit their old home and family very rarely, perhaps only once every year or two.

So how do the monks spend their time? Firstly, in every monastery, large or small, there are what we might call liturgical services, at least two or three daily, in the course of which there is a lot of chanting, accompanied by blowing of horns, banging of drums, and clashing of cymbals. It all creates a very powerful effect. Several times a day you sit for an hour or two at a time chanting the words of the sacred scriptures, perhaps the *Diamond Sūtra* or the *Heart Sūtra*, or invocations to the lamas, or praises of the Buddha, or summaries of the doctrine.

Then to the tremendous sound made by the booming of the great trumpets, the rattling of hand drums, and the higher register of clarinets when Buddhas and Bodhisattvas are being invoked, are added the extraordinarily deep bass voices of the monks. I once heard the Dalai Lama chanting in the Japanese Buddhist temple in Bombay, and his voice filled the whole place with perhaps the deepest human sound I have ever heard. He was only in his mid-twenties at the time, but his voice was so deep that when he chanted the mantras the whole place seemed to tremble, and people told me afterwards that they felt shivers going up and down their spines.

So imagine the effect when there is not just one person doing this, but a great throng of monks. Imagine, in the semi-darkness of a great hall, with massive Buddha-images at one end and thangkas on the walls, with incense burning and butter-lamps flickering, that along with the sound of musical instruments there are hundreds or even thousands of voices all chanting together in these very deep tones, sending a wave of sound rolling from every corner of the congregation. There is nothing quite like it for sheer volume and depth and intensity of sound. Just imagine participating two, three, four, perhaps even five times a day in this sort of liturgical meditation. You are swept along on a wave of sound. You hardly need to meditate; you just let yourself go. You may not be a very holy monk, you may not be a very bright geshe, you may not know your logic or your vinaya very well, but when you participate in this kind of service several times a day, it cannot fail to have an effect.

At other times, the monks may be chatting with friends, reading and studying in their cells, painting pictures, splitting wood in the monastery kitchen, ploughing or reaping in the monastery fields, or carrying great buckets of water up hundreds of stone steps. But whatever you are doing, when the trumpet sounds you drop everything and go into the shrine-room. When you do this week after week, month after month, year after year, until a point comes when you do not remember the time when you were not a monk, then obviously it all sinks in, it has its effect. Perhaps a third of the time in many monasteries is given over to these great chanting services, and all the monks – whether they are great spiritual masters, or cooks or carpenters – take part in them.

If they are intellectually inclined, the monks spend the rest of their time studying. They read the scriptures, go to their teachers for explanations, discuss among themselves, and practise formal debate. They also meditate, they teach if they are qualified to do so, and some of them follow various professions. In Tibet the doctors were mostly monks. There was a special medical college in Lhasa for training monk-physicians, who followed a mixture of the Indian and Chinese medical systems, including acupuncture.

In addition, they may be artists; most thangkas or painted scrolls were painted by monks. They may be carpenters, making the monastic furniture, or tailors, making not only the monks' robes but garments for lay people too. In this way they can earn a little money on the side; the Tibetans consider this quite acceptable. Of course the vast army of monks has to be fed, so there are also monk cooks and chefs preparing meals for hundreds or even thousands of monks every day. I remember once in Kalimpong a new restaurant opened, serving Tibetan, Chinese, and Indian food, and everybody started going there. I asked someone why it was so popular, and I was told that among the refugees recently arrived from Tibet were some of the best cooks from Drepung Monastery, and that they had taken on the running of this restaurant. Thus they were able to provide for themselves even though they were refugees.

Tibetan monks wear dark maroon robes, and these are the same regardless of rank or school (though the Nyingmapas' robes are of a slightly brighter and lighter shade). The three yellow robes of Indian tradition are also incorporated into the dress of the Tibetan monastic orders, though they are usually kept for ceremonial use only.

Thus far I have mentioned only monks. What about Tibetan Buddhist nuns? There are no fully ordained nuns, no bhikṣuṇīs, in Tibet, and there never have been. This ordination was not introduced into Tibet, apparently because there were never enough Indian bhikṣuṇīs in Tibet to form the necessary quorum. The nuns in Tibet are technically either *genyemas*, female probationers, or *getsulmas*, female novices, and there are not very many of them. In Kalimpong I met hundreds of Tibetan refugee monks but only a handful of nuns.

Tibetan nuns might live in a nunnery or *ani gompa* but there were also two other kinds of nun. First there were those from well-to-do families who lived at home rather than going into a convent. The family would set aside a special set of rooms, even a little cottage in the grounds of their property, for the daughter or sister or mother who had become a nun. Often a learned monk would visit regularly to teach her, but although she had her own establishment – her own kitchen, her own shrine – technically she was still living at home under the guardianship of her family. Owing to the rather unsettled social and political conditions that prevailed in Tibet for many centuries, often it was not safe for such women to live in any other way.

Then there were a number of wandering mendicant nuns, who may or may not have taken monastic ordination. Some of these were a bit rough and ready, but others were very pious, spiritual people, rather like the Indian female sādhus. There were also a few female hermits – nuns or lay women – who lived quite alone regardless of dangers, in the forest or in mountain caves, simply meditating like Milarepa. There was also one female incarnate lama, the famous Dorje Pagmo, who was the abbess of a monastery of 500 monks. Tibet was probably the only part of the Buddhist world where this could happen. Unfortunately the current Dorje Pagmo eventually defected to Peking and was last heard of broadcasting communist propaganda on the radio.

Lay Buddhists are numerous in Tibet, and often are no less sincere in their spiritual life than the monks and nuns. The strict lay followers observe the five *śīlas* or precepts; but most lay Buddhists are 'one śīla upāsakas' – they take only the first precept, which is to refrain from taking life. This is not because they consider the other precepts unimportant, but because in their view it is a great sin to take precepts and then break them. They therefore prefer to take only those which they are quite sure they will be able to observe. A few just take the three Refuges.

In my experience Tibetan lay people are extremely generous, in particular giving a great deal both in money and in kind for the support of their religion. In my early days in Kalimpong one of the Tibetans who studied English with me was a merchant from Kham in eastern Tibet, and he told me that people there usually gave one third of their income for the support, in one way or another, of Buddhism. They would divide their income into three equal portions. One third went on domestic and business expenditure, another third went on pleasure, that is to say picnicking, gambling, horse racing – the Tibetans are very fond of these things – and the rest was used for donations to monasteries, offerings to monks, ordering new images or paintings, after-death ceremonies, and so on.

Most Tibetan lay people, like the monks, regularly recite mantras. They have nearly all been initiated into a meditation on a Buddha or Bodhisattva, and they recite their mantras whenever they can. They may chant as they are walking along the road, or, when the day's work is done, a woman might sit on her doorstep quietly reciting mantras to herself. You can tell as you pass that they are quite absorbed. They do not do it mechanically; there is a great deal of religious feeling involved.

Every Tibetan Buddhist home has (or at least had) a domestic shrine with an image of the Buddha or one of the Bodhisattvas. This shrine, which occupies the place of honour in the sitting-room where visitors are entertained and guests put up for the night, is the focal point for the entire household.

Pilgrimage is another important part of Tibetan lay Buddhist life. There is still a great deal of the nomad in the Tibetans. They love to wander, to go on long journeys all over Tibet – even, in the past, all over India – visiting the shrines and holy places. They would also sometimes go into retreat and meditate. A man might entrust his family and business to his wife and spend three months in retreat, meditating and reciting mantras. Lay women are also very active in religious life, and are very much in evidence at all religious functions, celebrations, pujas, and so on. Often women take the initiative, having their own religious organizations, their own processions, their own meetings, even their own publications.

Tibetan Buddhists attach great importance to what we would call precedence – social, ecclesiastical, and spiritual. This is strictly observed on all formal religious occasions. Its importance for Tibetan Buddhists consists in the fact that it reflects the important principle of spiritual hierarchy. Inasmuch as the Dharma is a path there must be different stages on that path, different grades of attainment and realization. People can therefore be regarded as forming a hierarchy along these lines, and everything which they do, and which is done in connection with them, should reflect this hierarchy of stages of attainment. The Tibetans are therefore very particular about things to which we in the West would attach relatively little importance. For example, if you attend a religious ceremony in a Tibetan temple or monastery, you will notice that all the seats are graded. Towards the altar the seats are very high, perhaps six feet off the ground, like thrones; then they gradually become lower until you are perhaps just sitting on an ordinary mat. This is not done in accordance with any aesthetic principle, but with strict ideas of precedence and hierarchy. You can quickly tell how highly or otherwise the Tibetans esteem you according to the number of inches from the ground you are requested to sit.

Whenever I arranged Tibetan ceremonies at my vihara in Kalimpong I had to be very careful – especially when I invited certain high-ranking incarnate lamas – to make sure that everyone got the right kind of cushion, the right number of stripes of brocade, and so on. Protocol was really carried to a fine art. Even the tea cups, when tea was served ceremonially, would be graded from simple china cups, through more elaborate cups with lids and stands, right up to beautiful jade cups on silver stands. Eventually you might find yourself being served tea in an ancient jade cup on a solid silver stand, with a gold decorated lid topped by a magnificent jewel. Then you would know you had really arrived.

In accordance with this idea of precedence, the monks, and to a lesser extent the nuns, are – or were – treated with much reverence and devotion in Tibet. At the same time, the connections between monks and laity were very close. Every family had someone in robes, a son or brother who was a monk, so it was as though they had their own representative in the monastery. If another member of the family wanted to become a monk he would usually go to the same monastery, so that his uncle or brother could teach him. As well as this sort of link between the monks and laity, there is also the economic dependence of the monks on the laity, though this is perhaps less than it is for the monks of South-east Asia where it is seen as a disgrace for a monk to work, or even to do anything with his hands. It is not like that in Tibet, as we have seen.

The laity are for the most part dependent on the monks for spiritual guidance and advice. They often go to the gompas to visit and consult the monks, to attend pujas, to participate in processions,. or listen to lectures; and they often invite the monks to their homes. The monks are free to go out during the day, and can even get leave of absence for a few days or weeks to go to a lay person's house to teach, conduct services, and so on. Thus there is a constant coming and going between the houses of the lay people and the monasteries. The spiritual connection is much closer than in Theravādin countries, where the monks tend to be divided from the lay people rather sharply. The Theravādin view is that whereas the monk aims for Enlightenment, the lay person can aim only for a good rebirth, and this tends to produce a division, even a dichotomy, between the monks and the laity. But in Tibetan Buddhism all alike can aim for Enlightenment. Whether monk or lay, all Tibetan Buddhists accept the Bodhisattva ideal. They all believe they should aspire to gain Enlightenment for the sake of all living beings. Serious Tibetan Buddhists, both monks and lay people, in fact take the Bodhisattva ordination and the Bodhisattva vow – the vow to strive for Enlightenment not just for one's own sake but for the sake of all sentient beings.

Along with this vow, they may undertake to observe the Bodhisattva precepts, of which there are eighteen major and forty-six minor ones in the Tibetan tradition. These constitute a common factor in the spiritual life of monks and lay people in Buddhist Tibet. Indeed, we may say that the Bodhisattva precepts have helped to mould the whole character of Tibetan Buddhism. The first major Bodhisattva precept is very simple (simple to understand, that is, not easy to practise). It is to undertake not to praise oneself or disparage others. In one way or another we do this all the time, either individually or collectively; we always want to exalt ourselves and deprecate others. Thus we extol our own country at the expense of other countries, our own religion at the expense of other religions, or just ourselves at the expense of other people. So this first precept is about trying not to do this – and in fact Tibetans are very unwilling to criticize. It is particularly unthinkable for them to criticize someone else's religion.

Another of the major precepts is a warning not to instruct in the doctrine of *śūnyatā*, emptiness, anyone who is not prepared for it. Teaching must be adjusted to the psychological and spiritual needs of the person concerned. There is also a precept that enjoins us not to disparage the Hīnayāna. It may not be as fully developed as the Mahāyāna, but it is an indispensable stepping stone. You might as well say that the lower rungs of a ladder are less important than the higher rungs. Another precept consists in the determination not to give up the Bodhicitta, the will to Enlightenment for the benefit of all. However difficult things may be, however impossible other people may be, you must never give up the aspiration that one day they too will realize Enlightenment, will come to Buddhahood.

One of the minor offences for one who has taken the Bodhisattva vow is not showing respect for those who are one's seniors in Bodhisattva ordination. Another is to despise evildoers because you think they are less virtuous than you. They may be, but that is no reason to look down on them. It is also an offence to laugh heedlessly. This does not mean that you should not laugh, but if you are a Bodhisattva, or aspirant Bodhisattva, you should not do so mindlessly, without awareness. Another precept is that if someone in your vicinity is angry, you should try to pacify their anger. According to the Mahāyāna, anger is the worst of all mental states, so that if there is even a hint of it in our surroundings we should try to reduce it. Another offence is to neglect the sick – a very practical down-to-earth precept – and it is also an offence not to work for one's own circle of disciples and students.

These precepts illustrate the spirit of Tibetan Buddhism, the common ideal of monks and lay people alike. Whatever their differences in life-style, type of ordination, or level of spiritual attainment, the unifying factor of all Tibetan Buddhists is their reverence and devotion to the Bodhisattva ideal, the ideal of Enlightenment for the benefit of all.

ཨོཾ་མ་ཎི་པདྨེ་ཧཱུྃ། ཨོཾ་མ་ཎི་པདྨེ་ཧཱུྃ། ཨོཾ་མ་ཎི་པདྨེ་ཧཱུྃ།

ཨོཾ་མ་ཎི་པདྨེ་ཧཱུྃ། ཨོཾ་མ་ཎི་པདྨེ་ཧཱུྃ། ཨོཾ་མ་ཎི་པདྨེ་ཧཱུྃ།

5

Symbols of Tibetan Buddhist Art

We have seen that Tibetan Buddhism is a direct continuation of Indian Buddhism, that it is almost as if Indian Buddhism died in India only to be reborn on the soil of Tibet. Likewise, Tibetan Buddhist art is largely a continuation of the Indian Buddhist artistic tradition, particularly that of the Pala dynasty of eastern India in the eighth to twelfth centuries CE. Tibetan Buddhism continued that artistic tradition especially in its iconography, that is, in the depiction of images of Buddhas, Bodhisattvas, ḍākinīs, and so on. There is also some influence from Nepalese Buddhist art, but that tradition had itself been deeply influenced by the Pala tradition.

Chinese influence on Tibetan art is very secondary, and shows up mainly in matters of detail. For instance, if we look at *thangkas*, painted scrolls, we see that the iconography of the figures – their colours, the ritual implements they bear, their expressions and gestures, insignia and emblems – is all strictly determined by the Indian iconographical tradition. But when it comes to little details like the way in which the artist painted mountains, flowers, clouds, streams, or waterfalls, these reflect a definitely Chinese artistic tradition. We find a charming contrast between the Indian tradition, reflected in the iconography, and the Chinese influence, reflected in the natural objects – perhaps especially the clouds which are often very beautiful, with an effect of movement and iridescence which it takes a great deal of skill to capture. This Chinese influence is naturally more pronounced in the art of the areas of eastern Tibet adjacent to China itself. In the decorative arts also, the Tibetan tradition incorporates many Chinese motifs, such as the phoenix and the dragon. These symbolize, respectively, the yin and yang forces in the universe, and they are represented in Tibetan art as in Chinese art. Whether woven into carpets or carved into the woodwork of shrines, the Tibetan phoenix and dragon are exact replicas of their Chinese prototypes.

If we look more closely at the Indian and Chinese elements in Tibetan Buddhist art, we find that the specifically religious component of the art is Indian, whereas the secular component tends to be Chinese. Often these two aspects exist separately, side by side, but the best examples of Tibetan art display a perfect blending of the two. At its most perfect, Tibetan art is neither Indian nor Chinese, nor even both together, but uniquely and characteristically Tibetan. At the same time, however, the original Tibetan contribution is rather meagre. Tibetan Buddhist art draws its religious inspiration from India and its secular or more aesthetic inspiration from China, and although it fuses them into something distinctive and incomparable, it draws very little from purely indigenous sources.

This lack of originality brings us to perhaps the most important characteristic of Tibetan art. We speak of Tibetan *Buddhist* art, but strictly speaking this is a tautology. All Tibetan art is entirely Buddhist, or entirely religious; there is no secular art, or at least none worth mentioning. This is in accordance with the general pattern of Tibetan life, at least as it was before being disrupted by the Chinese occupation. The whole scheme of Tibetan life was based on certain traditional values, spiritual values, which had been handed down by way of a succession of teachers and disciples through the ages. All aspects of Tibetan life, therefore, inasmuch as they are related to these values in one way or another, also provide means of access to them. This applies to all areas of Tibetan life: economics, government, and administration, and even social customs and manners, as we saw with the idea of precedence in Chapter 4.

Because these aspects of life are closely interwoven with spiritual ideals, it is not surprising that Tibetan art and literature should be mainly religious. Apart from the Gesar epic, the Tibetans' only secular poetry, so far as I am aware, is a little book of love poems attributed to none other than the sixth Dalai Lama. Otherwise, their poetry is entirely religious. Similarly, there is no secular painting or sculpture. Where religious art does depict secular life, it is only in little details, for instance in some of the illustrations on the Tibetan Wheel of Life. Music, dance, and drama are entirely religious, apart from a little folk music and folk dancing. Even many of the applied arts such as woodcarving and metalwork are basically religious.

It is largely because its main function is religious that Tibetan Buddhist art is not very original in the modern sense. It doesn't even try to be original. A Tibetan Buddhist artist would in fact regard striving for originality as an aberration. He would be highly unlikely to decide spontaneously to paint his own idea of, say, the Buddha Amitābha. Instead, he will just sit in his studio or workshop until someone comes and orders a thangka of that particular Buddha.

If you do go along to order a picture, you don't get down to business straight away. That is not the way things are done. Polite enquiries about each other's health must be exchanged, and tea must be offered and drunk. Only then will the purpose of your visit be broached. The first question to be settled will be the rather prosaic one of the size of the thangka you want. The next question, usually, is whether you want gold to be used and, if so, how much – gold being charged for separately. When all this has been settled, you can get down to discussing the deity you would like to have depicted. If it is a well-known figure like Amitābha, the artist will know the iconography off by heart. Otherwise, if it is a more obscure figure, he will rummage in a drawer containing wood-block prints of a variety of figures – Buddhas and Bodhisattvas, ḍākinīs, dharmapālas, and so on. Eventually he will pull one out and ask, 'Is this the one you want?' If it is, then after your departure he will transfer the outline on to the rectangle of silk on which he will paint it.

In other words, the picture is executed according to the traditional iconography. The artist does not depict Amitābha according to his own ideas. Such things as proportion and colour, posture, and insignia, are all determined by tradition. There is some scope for originality, but it is very limited, on the whole being confined to the more secular and Chinese-influenced details, such as landscape, and to the offerings that are being made to the deity. A great deal of originality sometimes goes into these things. The better artists will, of course, produce finer works of art, but they still work within the tradition and will never try to paint the Buddha as they think he looked or ought to look.

The purpose of Tibetan religious art is not to give expression to the artist's own attitude or mentality. All the different forms of Tibetan art have one aim, which is to put the viewer, the individual Buddhist, in touch with what the Tibetan tradition calls the 'One Mind', the absolute consciousness, the *dharmakāya*, or Reality. If that is not possible, at the very least it aims to put the individual in touch with a higher, wider, and more comprehensive level of being and consciousness. Tibetan art does this with the help of symbols.

We can define a symbol as 'that which by custom or convention represents something else'. In other words, it has a meaning beyond itself, represents something other than itself. But in the context of Tibetan art a symbol is much more than this. It is not like the symbols of mathematics, not like, for instance, the letter *x* which represents the unknown quantity. A true symbol can be defined as an object or a phenomenon on a lower order of existence which stands for, represents, or takes the place of, a corresponding object on a higher order of existence. This definition of a symbol is based on the conception of a hierarchically ordered system of reality. For example, in some traditions the sun is regarded as a symbol of God, or, as in Plato's thought, a symbol of the Good. This is because the sun – the source of heat and light and therefore life – occupies a position in the physical world analogous to that of 'God' on the spiritual plane. The sun is a symbol not just in the sense of representing God, but in the sense that on its own level – the level of the physical world – the sun directly corresponds to that higher reality which is called God on the spiritual level. The same reality is being looked at from two different points of view, or within two different contexts.

The symbols of Tibetan Buddhist art are of this order. They are symbols by virtue of their place in a system of correspondences, based on a hierarchy of spiritual values in the universe as a whole. Though they themselves are material or mundane, they remind us of the existence of a higher order of being, and in a sense they even put us in touch with that higher order and enable us to communicate with and experience it. Symbols in this sense pervade all four of the principal categories of Tibetan art: architecture, paintings and iconography, ritual objects, and decorative arts. Here we will look in more detail at the first two of these.

ARCHITECTURE

One of the few indigenous Tibetan contributions to Buddhist art is its architecture. And one of the best-known and most wonderful examples of this is the Potala, the palace or monastery or temple – really all three combined – of the Dalai Lama in Lhasa. This was originally a secular building, a sort of castle of the Tibetan kings, but it was transformed by the great fifth Dalai Lama into something much more characteristically Tibetan. The Tibetan style of architecture was, of course, determined to a great extent by the climate. In Tibet one needs protection from the terrific winds and extreme cold. It was also influenced by the available materials; there is plenty of stone and rock for building purposes, but very little wood, Tibet being largely non-forested.

These two constraints determine some of the most distinctive features of Tibetan religious architecture. We find enormously thick walls, perhaps ten or fifteen feet thick, like European castle walls, to keep out the cold and frost and damp. Usually the lines are very simple, the basic pattern being of vertical walls that slope slightly inwards, and flat roofs. The most characteristic of all religious buildings, the monasteries or gompas, are very often situated high in the mountains, sometimes on crags or spurs of rock. A gompa rises out of the rock as if it were a natural growth of the mountain, as if it had grown straight out of the living rock. This is true above all of the Potala, but also of many temples and monasteries in Tibet. From a distance, they seem to be continuations of the mountains themselves.

This feature of Tibetan architecture is brought out in a number of paintings by Lama Govinda, who was not only a great writer on Buddhism but also a skilled artist. Many of his paintings depict these magnificent, rather barren and rocky Tibetan landscapes, with gompas – at heights many thousands of feet above sea level – 'growing' out of the mountains. This style of architecture seems to possess its own symbolic significance, acting as a reminder that the spiritual life is not 'stuck on to' the secular life. No, the one grows naturally out of the other as its culmination and perfection. Lama Govinda's paintings convey this impression very strongly indeed, but even in ordinary photographs of the great monastic shrines of Tibet one can see how their lines continue the lines of the mountains. This type of architecture is specifically Tibetan, owing nothing to India or China.

Another architectural feature of the Tibetan landscape is one of the most important and most ubiquitous of all Buddhist symbols: the stupa (*chorten* in Tibetan). This was originally a sort of funerary mound, a great heap of earth which enshrined the ashes of some great teacher or hero, a Buddha or arhant, or a universal king. The stupa is very prominent in Indian Buddhist art and architecture, but the Tibetans adapted it in their own way, as did the Buddhists of other countries. There are many different kinds of stupa in Tibet, but their basic structure is quite simple.

Essentially a stupa is made up of geometrical forms that symbolize the five elements: earth, water, fire, air, and space or ether (*ākāśa*). The earth element is symbolized by a cube. Just as a cube is very stable and can't easily be pushed over, so earth represents stability. It is the grossest of the elements, the heaviest, and so its representation, the cube, is the first element in the stupa. If you want to build a stupa you start by laying down a cube as the base.

On top of that is placed a sphere – or, more often, a hemisphere – which symbolizes water. The sphere is the least stable solid figure: just a touch and it will move. It is therefore an appropriate symbol for water, because unlike earth water always moves. It flows, it is unstable. On top of the sphere or hemisphere comes a cone. This represents fire – a cone is almost the shape of a flame – and it points upwards just as a flame points upwards as it burns.

Balanced on the point of the cone is a sort of bowl or saucer (which also looks like a crescent if depicted two-dimensionally). This symbolizes air, and is the inverted bowl of the sky or firmament. In the crescent or bowl is a flame tapering to a point, and this point, this position without magnitude, represents the so-called sixth element, consciousness. It is represented in this way because a point has no dimensions, just as consciousness itself, unlike the other elements, has no dimensions. Consciousness is that which 'contains' them all without itself being contained by anything. It is symbolized by that point, which indicates a transition from the physical or material plane to another dimension, that of mind or consciousness.

But why is this particular architectural form, the stupa, built up from symbols representing the five elements? Why should a chorten, a funerary monument, incorporate these symbols? The reason is related to the very fact that it is a funerary monument, built over the ashes of a dead person or in memory of them. The stupa is made up of the symbols of the elements because at the time of death the physical body, in fact the whole psycho-physical being, is resolved back into the elements from which it came.

At death, the solid parts of the body revert to earth. The fluid parts – blood and the rest – revert to water. The vital heat in the body returns to fire, being absorbed into the total heat and warmth of the universe. The air which fills our lungs is just exhaled into the atmosphere. When our physical body ceases to exist, the space it occupies merges into the great space. Finally, our mind also, when the bonds of the ego are dissolved – which is a sort of spiritual death – becomes non-different from absolute mind or absolute consciousness. This arrangement of the elements in the symbol of the stupa forms the basis of the Six Element Meditation, a traditional Buddhist practice designed to deepen one's insight into the constituents of the body and their dissolution at death.

Another architectural symbol is the three-storeyed temple. Many Tibetan temples are built with three storeys, which represent the three levels of existence, one of many ways in which existence can be divided, and one of the most ancient. The three levels are the mundane level, the archetypal level, and the absolute level. One finds enshrined on each storey an image of the Buddha, and these images represent the three *kāyas* of the Buddha. *Kāya* literally means 'body', but it is to be understood here more in the sense of personality. The three *kāyas* are the *nirmāṇakāya*, the created body; the *sambhogakāya*, the body of mutual enjoyment or glorious body; and the *dharmakāya*, the body of Reality. These three aspects represent the Buddha-nature itself as perceived at different levels of existence. When one perceives the Buddha-nature, the Buddha-being if you like, on the level of mundane historical reality, then one sees the historical Buddha. Going higher, one reaches the archetypal level, where one sees the same reality more closely, more truly, as the *sambhogakāya* Buddha, a sort of archetypal form. And if one goes higher still, then one sees the inner essence of those Buddha-bodies, the *dharmakāya*, or Reality itself, without any form.

Thus we find, on these three different levels, images of the Buddha representing the three *kāyas*. For instance, on the ground floor of the temple we find an image of Śākyamuni, the human historical Buddha: Gautama the Buddha, the Indian prince who lived around 500BCE and became Enlightened under the bodhi tree at the age of thirty-five. There he is, wearing his monk's robe, with his begging-bowl, and so on; and the walls of the ground-floor temple are covered with frescoes depicting incidents from his life. They show him sitting under the bodhi tree, resisting Māra the Evil One; giving his first teaching; and passing away under the twin sal trees. There are also very often stories from the Jātakas, the legends of his previous lives on the historical – or at least on the material – plane. All this represents the *nirmāṇakāya*. Or, as we saw in Chapter 2, in a Nyingma temple we might well find at this level an image of Padmasambhava, the 'second Buddha'.

But when we climb up to the middle floor it is rather different. Here we are in a different world, on a higher plane, and we find an archetypal Buddha enthroned. He wears not the ordinary monastic robe but princely garments of flowing, flowered silks, together with jewellery of various kinds. He is quite a different kind of figure, resplendent, archetypal, and glorified. On the walls we see nothing historical or human. We find, for example, mandalas, circles containing the principal archetypal Buddha forms. On this storey we find ourselves in the archetypal plane, above and beyond the human, historical world.

Then, climbing to the top storey, we find what is called the Ādibuddha, the primeval Buddha, the Buddha from the beginning, the Absolute Buddha. He is not represented wearing monastic robes, or even princely garments. He is represented without any clothes at all, and he may be blue, or black, or white, or dark brown; but in any case he is completely naked, because here all veils, all vestures, have been removed. This is the level as it were of Reality itself. Very often the Ādibuddha figure is in the *yab-yum* position, that is to say the male Buddha is depicted in sexual union with his female counterpart, symbolizing the fusion in the Enlightened mind of Wisdom, represented by the female, and Compassion, represented by the male. One finds these only at the top level because such yab-yum figures are regarded in Tibetan Buddhism as pertaining not to any lower mundane level, but to the highest and most spiritual level of all, the level of absolute Reality. Then on the walls, ideally, according to the best traditions, you find nothing: no form, no figure, not even a leaf or a flower. Apart from the Ādibuddha figure the room is completely bare.

In this way the architecture of the temple itself, including all its images, paintings, and decorations, symbolizes concretely these different levels of existence which one must ascend, from the historical reality at the bottom, through the archetypal or celestial reality, towards the Ultimate, the absolute Reality.

Paintings and Iconography

Another of the few indigenous contributions to Tibetan art is the remarkable colour sense of the Tibetans, as seen especially in their thangka paintings. The atmosphere of Tibet is remarkably clear, because at 12,000 feet or more above sea level the air becomes much thinner and more free of impurities. On emerging from the passes from India to Tibet, you find yourself in a completely clear, almost crystalline, atmosphere. If you are high enough up, you can see for scores, perhaps even hundreds, of miles. When everything is so transparent, so translucent and sparkling, then the sky is really blue. In the West we seldom see a really blue sky because we usually look at it as though through a sort of fog. But in the heights of

Tibet, above the level of smog and dirt and dust, you see how blue the sky can really be. And this is how the Tibetans see colours: they see a blue sky which is really blue, red rocks which are really red.

Lama Govinda once told me how astonished he was to open his eyes on a clear bright morning in Tibet and see rocks and mountains all around him which were so richly and brilliantly red that he couldn't believe his eyes. He even thought it was some sort of hallucination. But Tibet is really like that. When you look at the waters of a lake, they are a deep, vivid turquoise. When you look at the hundreds of miles of landscape, you see rich browns merging into beautiful purples. All around you are glowing colours.

It is because of this that the Tibetans have such a highly developed sensitivity to colour, and their art, particularly their thangka painting, reflects this. The best thangkas, those painted in the pure orthodox tradition, contain only organic and mineral pigments. Tibetan artists traditionally do not use prepared colours. They take earth, vegetable products, and semi-precious stones, and grind them and mix them for use as paints. Some, I am afraid, who have come into contact with Western civilization, are beginning to use ready-made paints, but the old artists, the traditional ones, still employ these natural colours. This helps them to create brilliant and really jewel-like effects. The best thangkas are remarkable for the sheer dazzling brilliance of their colouring. At the same time there is nothing loud or harsh about them, nothing that shrieks at you. The colours are brilliant, but at the same time soft and gentle: they seem natural and real.

The fact that the thangkas are so vividly coloured is connected with the purpose for which the paintings are intended. They are not just beautiful decorations to hang in your shrine; they are aids to visualization. They are painted in accordance with a particular tradition, which derives ultimately from somebody's meditation. Long ago, usually, a great mystic or yogi would have seen in his meditation a sort of divine vision, and described it to his disciples. He might have written about it, or even, if he was an artist himself, have painted or drawn it. Anybody else who wants to meditate upon that form or figure, that aspect of Reality, does so by means of a drawing or a painting deriving from the tradition which goes back to the original experience. (The actual process of visualization in meditation is described in more detail in Chapters 6 and 7.)

The vivid colours in which the thangkas are painted are themselves an important aspect of the symbolism of Tibetan art. The colour of a visualized form is often an important key to its significance. If you know what colour a Buddha or Bodhisattva is, then you already have some idea of his or her general spiritual significance. There are five basic colours in Tibetan iconography. Firstly there is red, a very deep, brilliant, rich vivid red. In the Tibetan Buddhist tradition, especially the Tantric tradition, red is the colour of love and compassion. If you see a red deity, a red Buddha or Bodhisattva, or a red ḍākinī, then you can be sure that the figure represents the Buddha-nature under the aspect of love or compassion. In the Tibetan tradition green is the colour of peace, calm, and tranquillity, and salvation from fear and danger of every kind. If you are rather anxious, if you worry a lot, then you should surround yourself with green; it will have a pacifying effect. Yellow – brilliant, vivid yellow – is the colour of growth, of prosperity and riches, even worldly riches, and of beauty and maturation. It is of course the colour of sunlight, the light which brings everything organic to a state of maturity. All this is represented by yellow in Tibetan iconography. Then there are two shades of blue, light and dark, both of which represent knowledge, that is, knowledge of the Truth, of the undifferentiated Absolute, knowledge of *śūnyatā*. This is represented by blue, the colour of the unclouded sky.

In addition to these colours, we also find black and white. As in many other traditions, white represents purity. It also represents primordial being, the absolute Reality that transcends time. Black, or very dark blue, symbolizes death and destruction, but in a very positive sense. A dark blue or black figure, usually with a wrathful expression, represents Enlightenment under the aspect of the destruction of spiritual ignorance.

Thus in Tibetan Buddhist art we can tell the general nature of a deity, whether Buddha or Bodhisattva, from the colour. If the deity is green, we'll know that it is connected with peace. If it is connected with love it will be red, if with purification white – or sometimes very pale blue – and so on. For instance, Green Tārā, a female Buddha form much loved by the Tibetans, is that form of Tārā which is concerned with pacification, and salvation from danger. Similarly the red Kurukullā, a rather extraordinary female Buddha figure, being bright red represents the love aspect, the passion aspect even, of the Enlightened mind.

The black or dark blue or brown figures are sometimes referred to by Western writers as demons or devils. Waddell, an early writer on Tibetan Buddhism, who was very well informed but didn't have much understanding, often used this sort of nomenclature, referring to the 'Buddha fiendesses' and the 'Buddha demonesses', but this gives quite the wrong impression. These figures are not demons or fiends or anything like that. They in fact belong to the highest level of all, the Buddha level, but as seen under the aspect of the destruction of spiritual ignorance. Sometimes they are very fierce indeed. Often they have thick dark strong bodies, wear garlands of skulls and elephant hides and tiger skins, and have long teeth or tusks and three or more eyes. They are very wrathful, they trample upon enemies, and have an aureole of flames. Though they look very fearsome, they are not demons and have nothing to do with hell in the Western sense. They symbolize those aspects of Enlightenment which burn up, overcome, and destroy ignorance in all its forms.

The point is that ignorance is so strong, so powerful, that the beautiful peaceful figures are unable to cope with it. They have to assume these terrible, wrathful forms in order to make some impression, at least, on the forces of ignorance, which otherwise don't take any notice of them. There are many legends to this effect, describing how a Buddha or Bodhisattva closed his eyes in meditation and out of his forehead emerged a great beam of light at the end of which appeared a terrifying monster, a wrathful figure brandishing a club and roaring 'I want your blood.' Apparently this is sometimes the only way in which the Enlightened mind can operate in this deluded world. When one confronts and surveys the world, one can feel every sympathy with this sort of approach. Perhaps it isn't the peaceful, meek and mild Buddhas and Bodhisattvas who are going to get anything done, but the more wrathful and terrifying ones.

However, one must always remember that this is not ordinary anger but what the Tantric tradition calls 'the Great Anger' or 'the Great Wrath'. Great, *mahā*, here means 'purified by *śūnyatā*', because it has passed through the fires of the Absolute. It is not an anger based on ignorance or on the ego; on the contrary, it is based on pure compassion, pure love. When ignorance and hatred encounter that love, they can experience it only as wrath or anger. This is the basis of this sort of symbolism in Tibetan Buddhism, especially in the Tantra.

There are, of course, also many peaceful symbolic forms in Tibetan iconography. One of the best-known and most popular is the eleven-headed and thousand-armed Avalokiteśvara (Chenrezi in Tibetan), the Bodhisattva of Compassion. This particular form represents absolute compassion, operating simultaneously in all directions and in all possible ways. The thousand arms represent the innumerable expedients of compassion, to help and save living beings, and it is significant that in each hand there is an eye, which means that even in the remotest operations of compassion there is awareness, or wisdom. There is a saying that it takes all the wisdom of the wise to undo the harm done by the merely good. The activity of compassion is not a sort of do-gooding, divorced from awareness or wisdom. Avalokiteśvara's eleven heads represent the eleven directions: north, south, east, west, the intermediate points, the zenith, the nadir, and the middle.

One of the most beautiful peaceful figures in Tibetan Buddhism is Green Tārā. As we have seen, her colour represents peace and salvation. Her left hand holds a lotus which has three blue blossoms – one quite open, one half open, and one just a bud. These represent the Buddhas of the three periods of time. It is as though Tārā manifests herself as these three Buddhas. The Buddha of the past is fully opened – he's gone, as it were, he has reached perfection. The Buddha of the present is half open, because his dispensation, his teaching, is still in force. The bud represents the Buddha of the future, who is yet to come. Green Tārā wears a tiara of five skulls or sometimes five jewels, representing the five wisdoms. She has two feet – which may not sound worth mentioning, but Tibetan Buddhist figures sometimes have ten feet, or sixteen, or more. One of her feet is in the lotus posture, which means that she is always in meditation. But the other is just hanging down, suggesting that she is ready to step out into the world.

We have only touched on a few of the symbols of Tibetan Buddhist art, but we can perhaps imagine the effect they have on the minds of people who are in touch with them all the time. In the West we suffer from a dearth of symbols. Often the nearest we get to a symbol is a Christmas tree. But the Tibetan Buddhist is, or was, surrounded by symbols. Wherever you looked, there would be a stupa, or a three-storey temple, or a thangka, or someone twirling a prayer wheel or telling their beads. Even Tibetan social customs and etiquette – the way people eat and drink and receive friends and visitors – have a symbolic value which helps to keep them in touch with that which is beyond the symbols, but to which the symbols point – higher levels of being and consciousness and reality.

Not all Tibetans understand the meanings of their symbols, but at least they have a sense of something greater, nobler, more spiritual, lying above and beyond and, at the same time, affecting them. Tibetan Buddhist art and its symbolism is therefore an important and vital aspect of Tibetan Buddhism. Our own lives in the West would be richer, and certainly more interesting, if they incorporated more symbolism of a spiritual nature. If we could follow the Tibetans' example and bring that about, perhaps we would be less estranged, less alienated, from reality.

ཨོཾ་མ་ཎི་པདྨེ་ཧཱུྃ། ཨོཾ་མ་ཎི་པདྨེ་ཧཱུྃ། ཨོཾ་མ་ཎི་པདྨེ་ཧཱུྃ།

ཨོཾ་མ་ཎི་པདྨེ་ཧཱུྃ། ཨོཾ་མ་ཎི་པདྨེ་ཧཱུྃ། ཨོཾ་མ་ཎི་པདྨེ་ཧཱུྃ།

6

THE FOUR FOUNDATION YOGAS

IN TIBETAN BUDDHISM, as in all Buddhist traditions, meditation lies at the heart of the spiritual life. Meditation has been part of Buddhism from the very beginning, going right back to the Buddha's own teachings. For example, the last three stages of the Noble Eightfold Path – Perfect Effort, Perfect Awareness, and Perfect Samādhi – are all concerned in one way or another with meditation. Samādhi or meditation is also the fifth of the six *pāramitās* or perfections, which, according to the Mahāyāna, form the path of the Bodhisattva. Not all schools of Buddhism have meditation as their main focus – it is Ch'an or Zen which specializes in it, while other schools may concentrate more on ethics or metaphysics – but for all schools meditation is a fundamental practice.

The details of the meditation experience differ greatly from one person to another depending on temperament, as well as on the kind of meditation one is doing, so it is not easy to generalize. But, very broadly, there are five successive stages of meditation, regardless of the Buddhist tradition we follow or the specific meditative path we pursue. These stages are not sharply demarcated from each other but, like the colours of the rainbow, fade into one another by imperceptible degrees.

The first stage can be described as withdrawal of the mind from the senses. Finding a quiet and secluded place, sitting still and closing our eyes, we gradually withdraw our awareness from the input of our physical senses until the mind is poised, as it were, in itself. But this is only the beginning of meditation.

The second stage is traditionally called the suppression of the five hindrances, the five kinds of negative emotional state which undermine our meditation and need to be dealt with if we are to make further progress. The first hindrance is 'craving for sensuous experience'. You may for a while shut out the external world – you are not looking at anything or listening to anything – but as you sit there, concentrated, a sort of tremor may arise in your mind, based on a recollection of a previous experience, and that will lead your mind almost insensibly back towards the original sense object. Along with that will come a desire for the experience of that sense object. This hindrance has deep roots that reach to the very depths of the unconscious mind. The second hindrance is hatred or ill-will or antagonism of any kind – irritation, indignation, and so on. Then there is 'sloth and torpor', physical sluggishness and psychological inertia, a sort of stagnation. Fourthly, there is restlessness and anxiety, or 'worry and flurry': a nagging sense of insecurity that won't let you settle down. The final hindrance is 'doubt and indecision'. This is not doubt in the sense of not being absolutely sure; as a hindrance, doubt is an unwillingness to commit oneself without being absolutely sure. So this stage of meditation consists in freeing oneself temporarily – under the special conditions of the meditation practice – from these five hindrances.

The third stage consists in elimination of discursive thought. Often people think that meditation is about getting rid of thought, and in a sense this is true, but with the proviso that you do not just eliminate thoughts or try not to have them. You just forget about thinking altogether, by taking a particular object of concentration and focusing all your attention on it. For example, in doing the Mindfulness of Breathing practice you concentrate on the breath, ignoring discursive thoughts and paying attention to the breath. You will then find – or rather won't 'find' because you won't even notice – that the thoughts are no longer there.

At first you may have to hang on to your concentration object, the breath, for dear life, vaguely conscious of a swarm of thoughts swirling all around you. But gradually you can relax your grip. Becoming more and more absorbed in the breath, you feel, rather than see, the wandering thoughts subside. They become faint and indistinct, and eventually die away altogether. But you are not thinking about the fact that you are not thinking. As soon as it occurs to you to think 'Oh look! I'm not thinking about anything,' your concentration slips and you have to start again. But when we eliminate discursive thought, the result is not a blank unconsciousness. We enter not a psychological vacuum, but a positive state of awareness in which the true nature of the mind, in its fullness and purity, begins to be revealed.

This brings us to the fourth stage of meditation: the development of higher states of awareness, new levels of consciousness. This experience comes naturally, almost of its own accord, as you become more and more absorbed in the object of concentration. Eventually you become as it were unified with it. You are not concentrating on anything in particular; you are just concentrated. Along with this comes an experience of increasing purity, peace, and bliss. You may have a sensation of being carried out of yourself, of being swept away. Sometimes, when this happens, it is a little frightening. It feels as if you are being borne along by a rushing river, and you don't know where it will take you. But if you resist giving in to the fear, the experience eventually passes away. We need to have faith in the nature of the experience, to surrender ourselves to it and let it carry us wheresoever it will.

The fifth and final stage is the arising of Insight, of direct knowledge of ultimate Reality. This represents a suffusion of our whole being with Reality in such a way that it is transformed and transfigured. At this point there is a qualitative change in our meditation experience: we start seeing into the heart of things, seeing things as they really are, more clearly than we had ever seen them in our lives before. It was said of the early nineteenth-century actor, Charles Kean, that to see him act was like reading Shakespeare by flashes of lightning. It is a little like that. At first we see just by flashes which for an instant illuminate the whole intellectual or spiritual landscape. Eventually the experience becomes more stable, the flashes last longer, and we start to take in more and more of the spiritual vista being revealed. It is as though a continuous beam of light gradually dawns, which we never again altogether lose. In this way, in the course of years or decades of practice, Enlightenment is attained.

These stages are common to all kinds of meditation practice, but there are many variations and the Tibetan tradition of course has its own particular approach. In Tibetan Buddhism meditation is mainly Tantric. We have seen in Chapters 1 and 2 that Tibetan Buddhism is triyāna in character, and that it derives its meditation from the Vajrayāna, which specializes in esoteric meditation and symbolic ritual. There are many methods of Tantric practice; indeed, the Tantra contains a bewildering profusion of material. However, we can distinguish between the foundation yogas, which are the preliminary practices, and Tantric meditation proper.

THE FOUR FOUNDATION YOGAS

The four foundation yogas or *mūla yogas* form the basis of Tibetan spiritual practice, and some acquaintance with them is crucial to an understanding of the spiritual life of Tibet. However much we may know about the Dalai Lama, or about Mahāyāna philosophy, if we have not caught the feeling of these practices then really we know nothing at all, spiritually speaking, about Tibetan Buddhism. The mūla yogas underpin as it were the whole vast fabric, the whole superstructure, of Tibetan religious life.

Mūla is a Sanskrit word, meaning literally root, or foundation. Just as if a tree's roots don't go deeply into the ground the tree will topple over when the wind blows, in the same way if the mūla yogas are weak, then the spiritual life which grows from those roots is weak and may also collapse. The four foundation yogas are therefore prefatory to the whole system of Vajrayāna meditation and religious observance. Tibetan Buddhism emphasizes that there is no success on the Tantric path if the four mūla yogas are neglected. You must practise them before you can think of embarking on the Vajrayāna.

In the West people are always looking for short cuts, and as soon as the Vajrayāna (or Zen for that matter) is mentioned, their ears prick up and they think: 'Here is a quick and easy path which circumvents all that meditation, asceticism, and study.' The truth is that the Tantra is a short path only if one practises it long enough, and an easy path only if one practises it hard enough. Tibetans often spend many years working on these foundation yogas, especially when they go into a 'long retreat' which traditionally lasts for a period of three years, three months, three weeks, three days, three hours, and three minutes. Most of us probably wouldn't get very far just sitting in a semi-darkened room and meditating indefinitely. After an hour or so we would be restlessly pacing up and down, wondering what to do next. But when the Tibetans go into this sort of retreat, they really get on with their practice, and in particular they get on with the four mūla yogas. I have met Tibetan monks who said that it was remarkable how quickly the time seemed to pass. The days, weeks, and months just slipped by because they were fully engaged in these practices. The more time they spent on them, the more deeply they went into them, the more interesting and fascinating they found them. Tibetan Buddhists, in short, are prepared to practise hard and to practise long.

In the West, unfortunately, we tend to be less patient. We want Enlightenment not at the end of twenty years' practice, but right here and now. And in a sense we are right to do so. But we can only get it here and now if we make a hundred per cent effort – which the very nature of our minds keeps us from doing. We tend to expect quick results from our spiritual life, neglecting the preliminaries. But these, if mastered, constitute half the battle. One could go so far as to say that if you prepare for meditation properly then you are already meditating. The end or aim of the spiritual life cannot be sharply separated from the means. Indeed, as Mahatma Gandhi once remarked, the end is the extreme of the means. If you devote yourself wholeheartedly to the means, then, almost without noticing, you gain the end. If you peg away at the preliminaries of the spiritual life, you will find yourself in due course deep in the heart of the essentials; but if you neglect the basics and try to leap ahead then you may not find yourself anywhere at all.

The word *yoga* literally means simply that which unites or joins. It is etymologically connected with the English word 'yoke'. In the West, yoga usually refers to a system of exercises. In Hinduism, it means any practice which unites one with Truth or Reality or God or, as in the more philosophical *advaita vedanta*, unites the lower self with the higher self by the recognition of their underlying non-duality.

But in the context of Tantric Buddhism the word yoga has a different meaning again. It refers especially to the union – both in the Enlightened mind and at all stages of the spiritual path – of Wisdom and Compassion, of supreme awareness of Reality and universal loving-kindness. It can also mean the union of the experience of emptiness, *śūnyatā*, and great bliss, *mahāsukha*. The Tantric tradition describes this kind of union by the term *yuganaddha*, usually translated as 'two-in-oneness' – the two-in-oneness of Wisdom and Compassion, or of emptiness and bliss. We could also speak of the two-in-oneness of saṁsāra and nirvāṇa, or of the Buddha and the Bodhisattva. This state of non-duality, this experience of unity in difference and difference in unity, is the highest goal of Tantric practice, and the mūla yogas are so called because they are practices which initiate the process of integration of one part of our nature with another. At the highest level this process culminates in the state of perfect integration of Wisdom and Compassion, of emptiness and bliss, which is Enlightenment itself.

The four foundation yogas therefore form the entrance to the Vajrayāna, or the Tantra, which, as we saw in Chapter 2, is the last of the three stages of development of Buddhism in India. The spiritual practices, the rites, the ceremonies, the meditation, and the symbolism of Tibetan Buddhism mostly come from the Vajrayāna. Although it incorporates all three yānas, in practice Tibetan Buddhism often starts straight away with the Vajrayāna, beginning with the four foundation yogas. This does not mean that the spiritual practices of the Hīnayāna and the Mahāyāna are neglected, for the most important of these practices are incorporated into the mūla yogas themselves.

The mūla yogas are practised in much the same way in all Tibetan Buddhist schools, though sometimes the order of practice is different and details may vary. The following summary accords mainly with the Nyingma tradition, the one with which I have had the closest personal connection.

THE GOING FOR REFUGE AND PROSTRATION PRACTICE

The mūla yogas begin where the whole Buddhist path begins, with Going for Refuge to the Three Jewels: the Buddha, the Dharma, and the Sangha. Going for Refuge is common to all schools of Buddhism, but the ceremony of Going for Refuge – 'taking the refuges' as it is often called – is not always taken very seriously. In India, for instance, the organizers of Buddhist public meetings sometimes insist that everybody recites the Refuges and Precepts even though the audience is mainly non-Buddhist and the meeting is itself political rather than religious. Such recitation has no real significance and in fact represents an abuse of tradition. In the Tantric Buddhism of Tibet, by contrast, Going for Refuge is not only taken very seriously, but is treated as an important spiritual practice in its own right. It is in this way that it figures in the mūla yogas.

The Going for Refuge and Prostration practice consists of three main elements: prostration, recitation, and visualization, corresponding to body, speech, and mind. In this way the whole being, the whole personality, is involved. This is characteristic of all Tantric practices. It is not enough just to do something mentally; you have to do it verbally and physically as well. In the case of the Buddha himself, these three modes of functioning correspond to the three *kāyas*. What in us are body, speech, and mind, are in an Enlightened being *nirmāṇakāya, sambhogakāya,* and *dharmakāya* respectively. (More is said about this in Chapter 7.)

The mental element of the first mūla yoga is the visualization of what is called the Refuge Tree. You start by sitting for meditation with your eyes closed. You see in your mind's eye a blue sky-like background, and against it, growing out of the water – or perhaps the mud – an enormous lotus-flower, in fact a whole lotus plant, as big as a great tree, with a thick central stem and four branches rising out of the stem in the four cardinal directions. At the top of each of these there blooms an enormous lotus flower. These lotuses can be any colour you like, but they must be enormous, and together they form a sort of mandala. When you have this great plant with its five blossoms firmly in your mind, and can see it quite clearly, then you direct your attention to the central lotus. You see layers upon layers of petals folded back, and right in the centre, sitting on the calyx of the central lotus, you visualize the founder of the particular Tantric tradition within which you are practising. For the Nyingmapas this is Padmasambhava, for the Gelugpas Tsongkhapa, and so on. You imagine this figure as clearly as possible, firmly seated in the middle of the central lotus, and you think of him as being the embodiment of all the Buddhas, the embodiment of your highest ideal in all its possible manifestations. All spiritual perfections, all qualities of Enlightenment, are concentrated in that one figure.

In the next stage you go a little further. You notice that the lotus has many tiers of petals, and underneath the central figure you visualize – sitting in rows on the tiers of petals – other lamas or gurus of the lineage, including your personal teacher and other masters from whom you have received instruction. Even lower down (still on the central lotus) you visualize the various Tantric deities – Buddhas and Bodhisattvas, both peaceful and wrathful – and underneath them the ḍākinīs and the dharmapālas. These figures represent the three Refuges under their more Tantric or esoteric aspect. The guru is the esoteric counterpart of the Buddha; the deities, archetypal symbols of spiritual experiences, are the esoteric aspects of the Dharma; and the ḍākas, ḍākinīs, and dharmapālas, the beings (or spiritual forces) in whose company one follows the path, represent the esoteric Sangha.

On the lotus blossom in front, the southern one, sits Śākyamuni, the human historical Buddha, along with other historical Buddhas, usually the Buddha of the past, Dipaṅkara, to the left and the Buddha of the future, Maitreya, to the right. On the lotus to the left (as you look at the tree) are the Bodhisattvas, usually the eight or ten principal ones including such figures as Avalokiteśvara and Manjuśrī. They represent the Sangha, the spiritual community, of the Mahāyāna. On the lotus to the north, behind the central lotus, one sees a pile of sacred scriptures representing the Dharma. To the right, on the eastern lotus, you see the assembly of arhants – those who are said to have gained liberation for themselves alone – who constitute the Hīnayāna Sangha. They include great Enlightened disciples of the Buddha such as Śāripūtra and Maudgalyāyana.

These images make up the main features of the Refuge Tree. The whole tree has to be visualized quite clearly and vividly before you begin the rest of the practice. You build up this mental picture, at the same time trying to develop a feeling of devotion for all these great spiritual figures and archetypal forms. Tibetans themselves are of course familiar with the appearance of the Refuge Tree from thangkas. So many figures are involved that the painting of even one such thangka may keep an artist busy for months on end, so thangkas of the Refuge Tree are not easy to come by. One was given to me once, but within a week it had gone. Tomo Geshe Rimpoche, who was a friend of mine, not only saw and admired it but remarked, rather thoughtfully, that he had no such thangka in his monastery in Ghoom, so that I had no alternative but to present it to him.

The verbal element of this mūla yoga consists in reciting aloud a series of verses expressive of one's Going for Refuge. One takes refuge in the founder of the tradition – Padmasambhava in the case of the Nyingma School – as the embodiment of all the Refuges.

Finally, there is the physical element of the Going for Refuge, as represented by the prostration. The body occupies an important place in the Vajrayāna as compared with the scant regard for it of the Hīnayāna. Of course all forms of Buddhism recognize that one cannot gain Enlightenment unless one has a human body, but despite this the body is often disparaged. Sometimes it is referred to as an animated corpse, or a bucket of filth that you carry around with you; all sorts of picturesque expressions of that kind are used. But in the Vajrayāna it is considered a great mistake to speak in dispraise of the human body, because it is the vehicle for emancipation and can become the body of a Buddha. Indeed, it is only through this physical body that one can gain Enlightenment. It is therefore viewed as rare and precious, something to be prized, and spiritual practice is seen as meaningless if the body does not play a part.

Religion must therefore be not just mental and verbal, but physical as well, and Tibetan spiritual life involves a great deal of bodily exertion. This is not just to keep you warm when there is snow outside your monastery. It is because the Tibetans believe that if the body is not involved, you are not seriously practising. This is why we find Tibetans doing things like prostrating themselves all the way from Lhasa to Bodh Gaya, a distance of five or six hundred miles. We might think this is crazy, but the Tibetans take it very seriously and they greatly respect people who do this sort of thing. In the same spirit, in the first mūla yoga you don't just visualize the Refuge Tree and repeat the formula of Going for Refuge; you also fling yourself down in a full-length prostration in front of the imagined Refuge Tree with all its lamas and deities and so on. In India abbreviated prostrations are more common but the Tibetans prostrate fully and rather dramatically, flat on their faces with their arms shooting out in front of them.

Having started by sitting and building up the visualization, you hold the completed mental image of the Refuge Tree while you rise from your seat, start reciting the Going for Refuge verses, and do the prostrations. In this way, the three elements of the practice – visualization, recitation, and prostration – come to be done simultaneously, which is quite an exercise in concentration and mindfulness. Body, speech, and mind co-operate: you keep the visualized Refuge Tree steady in your mind, repeat the verses, *and* fling yourself down. You also have to count your prostrations – which are traditionally done in multiples of 108 – either on your mala or by moving one of a pile of little stones every time you get up. The effect of all this is impossible to describe; you have to do it to know what it feels like. What one can certainly say is that it is good physical exercise. The Tibetans believe that it's a certain cure for tuberculosis, provided you do it long and energetically enough.

According to tradition you do 100,000 prostrations. This takes about three months if you do it full-time, but if you do just a few hundred a day it takes nearly a year to complete. The important thing is to do as many as possible. You can in fact take up other Vajrayāna practices before you have finished the preliminary practices, so that you are adding to your total of prostrations while at the same time embarking on a meditation on Tārā or Manjuśrī, or even on a more advanced practice. This may be a concession to the corruptions of modern times, but it is what the Tibetans themselves do.

The Going for Refuge and Prostration practice represents the 'Hīnayāna' component of the four mūla yogas, though this component is transformed by the general Vajrayāna context within which it takes place. Indeed, Tibetan Buddhism regards the whole of the Hīnayāna, or what we may call Basic Buddhism, as being summed up in the Going for Refuge to the Buddha, Dharma, and Sangha.

THE DEVELOPMENT OF THE BODHICITTA

The second mūla yoga is the arising of the Bodhicitta, the will or urge towards Enlightenment for the benefit of all living beings. To bring this about, we need firstly to develop love and compassion for all beings. This aspiration of course reverberates throughout the whole of Buddhism, but here as elsewhere the Tibetans add their own particular flavour, their own particular colouring. They suggest that one should regard all living beings as if they were one's own parents. Like most Buddhists, the Tibetans believe in rebirth, and they take this to its logical conclusion. (Tibetan Buddhists are rather fond of carrying things to their logical conclusions, so far as Buddhism is concerned.) They believe that we have each lived on this earth thousands or even millions of times, and that therefore, if we look far enough back, it is practically certain that everybody we meet has at some time, ten or a hundred or a thousand lifetimes ago, been our mother or our father. It's as though we have not just one set of parents, but millions of them.

To us in the West, even if we are Buddhists, and even if we accept – with more or less reservation – the idea of rebirth, it is not really part of our being. But in the case of the Tibetans it is in their bones and their blood, as it were, and they feel it very strongly. They actually believe that every single person they meet has been, at some time in the remote past, related to them as their mother or father, and therefore that they should be kind and affectionate towards them and treat them well. The Tantric tradition emphasizes that inasmuch as you have this degree of love and compassion for all sentient beings, you should naturally resolve to deliver them from suffering.

The Tibetans illustrate the point in the following way. Happening to walk through the bazaar, you notice that in one corner a disturbance of some kind is going on. Quite a crowd has gathered, and in the middle of the crowd someone is being kicked and beaten. Out of curiosity you draw near, and see that it is a woman – an old woman – who is being assaulted. Feeling somewhat concerned, and thinking that perhaps someone should intervene, you elbow your way through the crowd and discover, to your horror and astonishment, that it is your own mother who is lying there on the ground with blood streaming from her head. At once your attitude of impersonal civic concern is transformed into one of intense love and compassion and you rush forward to help, for the person who is suffering is near and dear to you.

The spiritual masters of Tibet say that if you can see each suffering being as your own mother or father, or as someone else who is near and dear to you, then compassion will well up in your heart – otherwise not. This is why they emphasize the idea. We see so much suffering in the world. We read in the newspapers of people being killed in accidents or disasters, or being slaughtered in their thousands in war, but so often we just turn to the next page and read the sports results. We think nothing of such horrors, because no one near and dear to us is involved. But if we feel as if all living beings are deeply and intimately related to us, if we act as though all beings are in fact our own reincarnated mothers and fathers, then compassion arises. Seeing all the suffering beings around us in this light, we will feel a tremendous urge to deliver them, to lead them on the path to Buddhahood. Moved in this way, we will resolve that through our practice of the Vajrayāna we will gain Enlightenment for the benefit of all living beings. In this way we are led to take the Bodhisattva vow.

The second mūla yoga consists in the repetition of a formula expressing this vow, this determination to gain Enlightenment not just for the sake of one's own emancipation, but for the welfare of the whole world of sentient beings. And it is to be recited 100,000 times. It is a characteristic feature of the Vajrayāna that you do a practice 100,000 times. This is because it needs to penetrate into the unconscious mind. It is no use just repeating something once and then thinking we have understood it and can put it aside. It is all too easy to say 'I vow to gain Enlightenment for the sake of all sentient beings' and think we have taken the Bodhisattva vow. But just *saying* the words may have made no impression whatsoever, not even a scratch on the surface of our mind. Hence the Vajrayāna exhorts us to go on repeating it, a thousand or ten thousand or a hundred thousand times. Maybe when we have done it a hundred thousand times, the meaning will begin to percolate below the level of the conscious mind and permeate the unconscious mind, which is what really matters.

Furthermore, between one's sessions of practice one should reflect that with every incoming breath the sins of all beings, all their weaknesses and imperfections, are entering one's body and are being absorbed into, and annihilated by, the Will to Enlightenment one has developed. Then one should imagine that with every outgoing breath, one's own good qualities, such as they are, are falling upon others like moonlight, and conferring happiness upon them. In other words one should feel that one's influence upon others is beneficent and positive, like moonlight. The comparison recalls Indian tradition, because in India, after the heat of the day, the moonlight is cool and soothing. If you practise the mūla yogas you have to ask yourself whether this is the kind of effect you have on others, and whether your friends would compare you with moonlight.

Besides doing this practice one should also cultivate the *brahma vihāras*, the four sublime states of love, compassion, sympathetic joy, and equanimity. These practices are common to both the Hīnayāna and the Mahāyāna; however, in general this mūla yoga, the development of the Bodhicitta, represents the Mahāyāna component of the four foundation yogas.

The Meditation and Mantra Recitation of Vajrasattva

The third mūla yoga is purely Tantric, with no real counterpart in the Hīnayāna or Mahāyāna. It is undertaken for what the tradition calls 'purification of sins', and the Vajrayāna attaches great importance to this. While its conception of sin is very different from that of Christianity, it recognizes that our minds are obscured by all sorts of things that we would rather forget about. If we are to get anywhere with our spiritual practice, however, we cannot forget about them; we have to drag them all out into the light of day, into the light of the Buddha, and resolve them. We have to recognize them clearly and face up to them before they can be purified. The Vajrasattva yoga, as it is also called, is undertaken for this purpose.

Vajrasattva's name means 'the Diamond (or Adamantine) Being'. Though a Buddha, he is represented iconographically in the form of a Bodhisattva, that is to say, as a young man wearing princely garments, jewellery, and other ornaments. Sometimes he is called the sixth Buddha, the esoteric or hidden Buddha. The Tantric tradition speaks of a sixth Buddha much as we might speak of a sixth dimension. It implies something mysterious, a sort of 'x-factor' which we do not really apprehend. Vajrasattva is the sixth Buddha in relation to the scheme of the five Buddhas, who are the transcendental counterparts of the five skandhas, the five constituents of conditioned existence.

In Buddhism the whole of existence is viewed as having two aspects: that which is conditioned, called saṁsāra (i.e. all that is depicted in the Tibetan Wheel of Life) and that which is Unconditioned, called nirvāṇa. Conditioned existence, the whole mundane universe both material and mental, consists of the five skandhas: form, feeling, perception, volition, and consciousness. On the Unconditioned or transcendental plane there is a corresponding division into the five archetypal Buddhas, often depicted in a mandala with one in the centre and one at each of the four cardinal points. The usual arrangement is to have the white Buddha, Vairocana, in the centre; then to the north the green Amoghasiddhi, to the south the yellow Ratnasambhava, to the west the red Amitābha, and to the east the dark blue Akṣobhya (though he is sometimes in the centre, with Vairocana to the east). The central Buddha is a synthesis of the other four, which represent special aspects of the main figure. Vajrasattva is the esoteric aspect of the central or fifth Buddha. We can imagine him as being behind the central Buddha in a different dimension, as it were, 'outside' the plane on which the five Buddhas are differentiated.

One of the fundamental principles of the Tantra, and of Tibetan Buddhism generally, is that all the Buddhas, Bodhisattvas, ḍākas, ḍākinīs, dharmapālas, and so on are to be found within one's own mind. If you penetrate right into the depths of your mind, beyond your ordinary conscious mind into something far greater, far higher and wider, then you encounter these forms and figures. And if you go deep enough into your own mind, beyond all thoughts, words, and deeds, even beyond all the other Buddhas and Bodhisattvas, you encounter the fundamental intrinsic purity of Vajrasattva. He symbolizes the primeval, original purity of one's own mind, its transcendental purity beyond space and beyond time. In other words, Vajrasattva represents the truth that whatever you might have done on the phenomenal plane, whatever sins you might have committed, however low you might have sunk on the scale of being and consciousness, in the depths of your being you are pure. Your true nature remains untouched and unsullied. Obviously this can be misunderstood. The fact that your basic mind remains pure does not mean that it doesn't matter what you do. It matters very much, because it is only if you behave ethically and develop Insight that you can realize the primordial purity of your own mind that is symbolized by Vajrasattva.

The purpose of the Vajrasattva practice is therefore to reintegrate us with our own innate purity, to purify us of our sins by the recognition that underneath the sins the immaculate purity of our own mind has never been tainted. Above and beyond all Buddhas and Bodhisattvas, above and beyond all worlds and universes, all thoughts and ideas, even all realizations and experiences, outside time altogether, our own mind remains absolutely pure. We acknowledge our sins as sins on their own level, but we purify ourselves by realizing that in the depths of our being we have never sinned. This is the essence of the practice.

The practice begins with another visualization. You visualize Vajrasattva immediately above your head. He is a brilliant white, like sunlit snow, and is sometimes without either garments or ornaments, sometimes clad in silks and jewels. He is youthful – the texts say sixteen years of age, which is supposed to be the ideal age so far as beauty is concerned – and he is smiling. You then visualize the *bīja* or seed syllable *hūṁ*, blue in colour, at the centre of his heart. This is surrounded by the circle of letters of the hundred syllable mantra of Vajrasattva. The letters stand upright, rather like the stones at Stonehenge, all white and emitting light.

A stream of milk-like nectar then descends from the seed syllable in the heart of Vajrasattva, as well as from the surrounding letters of the mantra. Descending into you through the top of your head, it goes right through your body, washing away all sins. You both visualize and experience this. With practice you can actually feel a sensation of coolness flowing down into the whole body and permeating it. Eventually your body becomes like a crystal vase filled with curds – the traditional comparison – and you feel cleansed and purified. You feel transparent like crystal, or even like pure light. (In fact, all visualization exercises have this kind of psychological effect.)

These are the main features of the visualization. Having done it, you then recite the hundred syllable mantra as many times as you can at one sitting, the aim being eventually to recite it 100,000 times. The mantra itself expresses the idea of re-integration with one's intrinsically pure Vajrasattva nature. At the end of the practice the visualized Vajrasattva is dissolved back into the void, into *śūnyatā*, which is the usual procedure at the end of any visualization exercise.

THE OFFERING OF THE MANDALA

The word mandala – literally 'circle' – has several meanings. In this context it means a symbolic representation of the entire universe according to ancient Indian cosmological tradition. The practice consists in offering this mandala, offering the cosmos as it were, to the three Jewels – the Buddha, the Dharma, and the Sangha – in both their exoteric and esoteric aspects. These are visualized more or less as in the Going for Refuge and Prostration practice except that here there is no tree. One then performs a special Tantric version of the devotional practice known as the Sevenfold Puja, after which one builds up and offers the mandala as a symbol of the universe.

This symbolic representation of the universe is made up of thirty-seven parts, representing prominent features of the universe as well as its most precious contents, including Mount Meru (the central mountain), the four major and eight minor continents, the 'seven precious things', and so on. The traditional practice is to construct it by heaping up grains of rice on a circular copper base and adding rings of copper or silver until one has built up a conical structure with several tiers. The various heaps of rice, around the foundation and at higher levels, represent different elements of the physical universe and one bears these in mind and repeats their names while building up the model. There are several ways of offering the mandala. Usually one lifts it up in one's hands, at the same time reciting various mantras and verses expressive of one's offering of the entire universe to the Three Jewels.

The meaning of the practice relates back to the second mūla yoga, whose aim is the development of the wish to gain Enlightenment for the sake of all beings. In order to do this, one needs an enormous accumulation of 'merit' or *puṇya*, in other words, good qualities and auspicious spiritual attributes. It is axiomatic for Buddhism that merit is gained by *dāna*, by giving. This is the basic, cardinal virtue. It is one of the most wonderful features of life in Buddhist countries that people are so generous, readily sharing with you whatever they have. If you visit someone's home, you will be offered at least a cup of tea, perhaps a whole meal, or a small gift. Similarly, you yourself must not go to see someone empty handed. So if it is meritorious just to offer a cup of tea or a little money, or to give one's time or energy, or even to offer a monastery or a temple, how much more meritorious it would be to offer the whole universe! If you offered absolutely everything, you would gain incalculable merit.

The problem is that we don't have at our disposal as much as we would like to offer, and many of us are quite poor. But Buddhism teaches that it is the intention that counts. The mental offering is in fact the real offering (with the proviso that one's offering is more likely to be real if it is accompanied by a physical act of giving). You offer this symbolic representation of the whole universe in all its aspects, with all its treasures, and at the same time try to develop the attitude that if everything was yours you really would offer it all to the Buddha, the Dharma, and the Sangha.

This must not become a mere formality. While offering the mandala, you should genuinely feel that you are offering up absolutely everything, that even if you became the richest person in the world you would devote it all to Buddhism. If you became master of the universe, you really could think of nothing better to do with it than to offer it to the Three Jewels. Some Buddhist kings actually used to offer their kingdom to the Buddha in a rather spectacular way (though sometimes they took it back again the next day). The offering of the mandala signifies the will to give, the will to surrender. It is the longest of the mūla yogas to complete, but the whole procedure should be done, as one would expect, 100,000 times.

Together, these four foundation yogas form the basis of Tibetan spiritual practice. They are regarded as preparatory to the practice of the Vajrayāna, of Tantric Buddhism as a whole, but it is also said that if any one of them – especially the Vajrasattva yoga – is practised sufficiently thoroughly, frequently, and sincerely, it will bring one very close indeed to Enlightenment.

ཨོཾ་མ་ཎི་པདྨེ་ཧཱུྃ། ཨོཾ་ཨ་མི་དེ་ཝ་ཧྲཱིཿ ཨོཾ་མ་ཎི་པདྨེ་ཧཱུྃ།

ཨོཾ་མ་ཎི་པདྨེ་ཧཱུྃ། ཨོཾ་མ་ཎི་པདྨེ་ཧཱུྃ། ཨོཾ་མ་ཎི་པདྨེ་ཧཱུྃ།

7

Tantric Initiation

It is clear from the details of the mūla yogas that Vajrayāna methods of meditation differ in many respects from those of the Hīnayāna or Mahāyāna. However, Tantric meditation is not defined by its practices. Its essential feature is that it is practised by the *sādhaka*, the practitioner, after initiation by a guru. This does not just mean being taught the method of meditation, although in a sense that is an initiation. The Sanskrit term for a Tantric initiation is *abhiṣeka*, the dictionary meaning of which is 'a sprinkling'. It is true that in the course of the initiation the person being initiated is sometimes ceremonially sprinkled with water. But this is just an aspect of the ritual: it does not tell us anything about the essential meaning of the initiation. The word the Tibetans use for *abhiṣeka* is *wongkur* (*wong* for short), and it gives us more of a clue as to what Tantric initiation really implies. *Wong* means 'power', 'energy', or 'spiritual potency', and *kur* means 'transmission' or 'bestowal'. So *wongkur* – transmission of power – renders the inner meaning of the word *abhiṣeka* rather than its dictionary definition. A Tantric initiation is essentially a transmission of spiritual power from the guru to the disciple. This is symbolized by the sprinkling of water, and very often embodied in a mantra, a sacred syllable or phrase to be repeated over and over again, which is given at the time of initiation.

On the other hand, we may prefer to think of *wongkur* in terms of the *activation* of power. The guru does not so much literally give some of his own power to the disciple as activate by his spiritual presence the latent spiritual forces of the disciple. But it must be said that in the course of a Tantric initiation many people do experience an actual transmission of power. They do not feel that something is being activated within them, but rather that something is passing into them from the guru, piercing them like a spiritual electric shock. Anyone who has experienced spiritual healing should be able to understand the sort of thing that is going on here. Not that Tantric initiation is in any way akin to spiritual healing; but just as a health-giving, positive force manifestly passes from the healer to the patient, so, on a much higher level, a kind of charge of spiritual energy passes from the guru to the disciple.

It is evident from this that Tantric meditation cannot be practised without a guru; this would be a contradiction in terms. If one practises an allegedly Tantric meditation without having been appropriately initiated by a guru, then it becomes a Mahāyāna meditation. On the other hand, if what is technically a Mahāyāna type of meditation is practised after initiation by a guru, it becomes a Tantric practice. We cannot categorize specific meditation practices as either Tantric or non-Tantric; the distinction depends entirely on whether you practise them after having been initiated, in the Tantric sense, by a guru. If you practise a meditation technique on your own, even though a book may label it Tantric, it is not a Tantric practice at all. So while there are in Tibetan Buddhism a number of meditation practices which are never (or never should be) practised without initiation, and might be described as Tantric meditation proper, they are 'Tantric' not on account of what you do in the course of them, but on account of the fact that you are initiated into them by a Tantric guru.

Broadly speaking there are four different 'wongs' or Tantric initiations in the Vajrayāna. First there is the *kalaśa abhiṣeka* or 'jar initiation', so called because in ancient India a jar was used in the course of this initiation (which consists of six minor initiations). Second is the *guhya abhiṣeka*, the 'secret – or esoteric – initiation'. This is so called because it includes, among other things, the practice of various esoteric methods of control of the breath and of the nervous energy. The third initiation is called the *jñāna-prajñā abhiṣeka*, which means 'the knowledge of *prajñā*'. *Prajñā* generally means 'wisdom', but in the Vajrayāna every term has a rather different meaning from its Mahāyāna definition. In this context *prajñā* means the female partner in the practice, also called the ḍākinī. This can be understood literally to mean a person with whom one performs various practices belonging to this level of Tantric meditation experience. Transposed into a lower key, so to speak, it can also be understood as representing what we may call the unrealized 'feminine' side of one's own nature in the case of a man, or the 'masculine' side in the case of a woman. Knowledge of this is the aim of the *jñāna-prajñā*. The last initiation is not usually given a descriptive title, but is called simply 'the fourth'.

These Tantric initiations are correlated with body, speech, and mind, the basic division of the human being in Buddhism. The aim of the Vajrayāna, as of all forms of Buddhism, is Enlightenment; but the Vajrayāna speaks of Enlightenment in a particular way, in terms of the acquisition of the three *kāyas*. *Kāya* literally means 'body', but not body as opposed to mind; 'personality' would be a better rendering. According to general Buddhist teaching, the three *kāyas* represent different facets of the Enlightened mind, different aspects of Buddhahood as it appears on three levels. First there is the *nirmāṇakāya* or 'manifested personality', in other words Buddhahood as it appears on the human historical plane in the form of the specific historical teacher, Gautama the Buddha (or Padmasambhava in the case of the Nyingmapas). Then the *sambhogakāya*, which literally means 'the body of reciprocal enjoyment', or 'the glorious personality', represents Buddhahood appearing on higher celestial or archetypal planes, above and beyond the historical context. Thirdly there is the *dharmakāya*, 'the absolute personality', or 'the body of truth'. This is Buddhahood in its ultimate essence, above the historical plane, and even above the archetypal plane.

So, the doctrine of the three *kāyas* is that the Buddha manifests or exists on these different levels of reality: the absolute level, the archetypal level, and the human historical level. The three *kāyas* also represent the body, speech, and mind of the Buddha. What in us is mind, in the Buddha is transformed into *dharmakāya*. What in us is speech, communication, in the Buddha becomes *sambhogakāya*. And what in us is physical body, in the Buddha becomes *nirmāṇakāya*. The object of the Vajrayāna is not just that we should gain Enlightenment in a general way. It is more concrete, more specific than that. The aim of the Vajrayāna is that we should become endowed with the three *kāyas*. Our body, speech, and mind should be transformed into the threefold personality of a Buddha.

The first three Tantric initiations and their associated practices are designed to bring this about. Our physical body is transmuted into the *nirmāṇakāya* of a Buddha with the help of the 'jar' wong and its associated meditations; our speech, our communication, is transformed into the *sambhogakāya* with the aid of the 'secret' wong, and our mind is transformed into the *dharmakāya*, the essence of Buddhahood, by means of the 'knowledge of *prajñā*' wong. The fourth wong represents the transmutation of body, speech, and mind, not just individually but collectively, into what is called the *svabhāvikakāya*, which means the 'self-existent body' or 'self-existent personality'. This is not really a fourth *kāya* but represents the collective transformation of body, speech, and mind into the three *kāyas* of a Buddha. Thus the fourth wongkur is itself not so much a separate wong as the totality of the other three.

The four Tantric initiations are also correlated with four yogas – not the mūla yogas, but quite different yogas sometimes known as the 'four tantras'. The first of these is *kriyāyoga*, the ritual tantra, which covers a whole class of practices, hundreds of different exercises. *Kriyāyoga* practice is usually described as consisting of one part meditation and three parts symbolic ritual. If a Tantric practice consists of, for example, a quarter of an hour's meditation and three-quarters of an hour's ritual, then it would be regarded as belonging to the *kriyāyoga*. The second yoga is the *ubhayayoga*, which means 'both sides' tantra, *ubhayayoga* practices being half symbolic meditation and half ritual. Thirdly there is what is called simply *yoga tantra*, which consists of three parts meditation and one part symbolic ritual. Fourthly there is the *anuttara yoga*, the unsurpassed yoga, which according to the traditional schema is devoted solely to meditation.

The correlation of the four initiations and the four yogas is not quite straightforward: there is not one initiation for each yoga. The first three yogas collectively comprise what is called the Outer or Exoteric Tantra, and the *anuttara yoga* comprises the Inner or Esoteric Tantra. If you want to practise anything belonging to the first three yogas, the Outer Tantra, you only need a simplified form of the first initiation, called the 'body' wong or 'little' wong, and then you can go ahead with the practice. But if you want to practise the meditations of the Inner or Esoteric Tantra, then you need all four initiations, which are collectively called the 'great' wong or the 'great Tantric initiation'.

Obviously there are limits in terms of space to what can be said about Tantric Buddhism in a few pages. But there are also limits in terms of appropriateness, or even propriety. In fact one of the conditions of initiation into the Inner Tantra is that you do not talk about its practices to anyone who has not received the same initiation. In any case, Tibetan Buddhists rarely talk or write about meditation – they're too busy practising it. It is only in the West that we have a lot of lectures and books on meditation. Of course there is no harm in having a sound knowledge of the theory, but sooner or later we have to start practising.

Though it is impossible to speak about the practices of the Inner Tantra, the Outer Tantra is more open and accessible. Its practices are followed by many lay people in Tibet as well as by the ordinary monks, those who are not teachers. There are many types of practice. When I myself first came into contact with Tibetan Buddhism, especially with Tantric meditation, I was bewildered by the profusion – even confusion – of material I found myself presented with. Having perhaps a rather methodical and tidy mind I wasn't quite happy with all these heaps of unorganized material that didn't seem to fit together in any neat fashion – until it became clear to me that it was never meant to be reduced to any sort of order at all. So probably the best thing I can do here is select one particular practice out of the heap, as it were, and concentrate on that.

One of the most popular practices of the Outer Tantra is the meditation on Green Tārā, Drölma in Tibetan. In the Hīnayāna and Mahāyāna, Buddhas and Bodhisattvas are always male, but in the Vajrayāna we find just as many female ones, and Tārā is the most prominent of these. Her Sanskrit name means, literally, 'the one who ferries across', in the sense of the one who saves, and it is usually translated 'the Saviouress'. Each Bodhisattva form represents one particular aspect of Enlightenment, and Tārā is the embodiment of compassion. More than that, we could say that she is even the embodiment of the embodiment of compassion, because she is in a sense the spiritual daughter of Avalokiteśvara, the great Bodhisattva of compassion. He is one of the three main Bodhisattvas of both the Mahāyāna and the Tantra, along with Manjuśrī representing wisdom and Vajrapāṇi representing power or energy.

According to legend, once upon a time Avalokiteśvara looked out over the world from the terrace of his palace and saw the whole mass of humanity. He saw people enduring so many troubles, so much suffering. Some were engaged in protracted lawsuits, some were lying sick on their beds, while yet others were being attacked by robbers and highwaymen, or suffering bereavement, or dying painful deaths, even being devoured by wild animals. When he saw the great mass of human misery, the great Bodhisattva Avalokiteśvara, out of compassion, could not help shedding tears. In fact he shed so many tears that a great lake formed. And in the midst of the lake appeared a huge white lotus, and when its petals opened, out came a beautiful green goddess – the Bodhisattva Tārā, born, the legend says, out of the tears of Avalokiteśvara. So if Avalokiteśvara represents compassion, Tārā is as it were the essence, the quintessence, of compassion.

In Tibet she has many forms, but there are two principal ones, White Tārā and Green Tārā. They are both highly revered, but Green Tārā – also called the Khadiravaṇī Tārā – is the more popular of the two. There are many ways of meditating on her, but the following is the standard evocation of Green Tārā. The general procedure is similar in other Tantric practices which evoke different Buddhas and Bodhisattvas.

The meditation has ten stages. As with any Tantric meditation practice, you start off by Going for Refuge, as a brief recapitulation of the Hīnayāna. But the refuges are given a Tantric colouring. First you say 'To the guru for refuge I go', because the Tantric view – as we saw in Chapter 4 – is that it is only through the guru that you can really come to know the other refuges. In this practice the guru refuge is Amitābha, the Buddha of Infinite Light, because he is the head of the spiritual 'family' to which Avalokiteśvara and Tārā belong. Tibetan paintings of Green Tārā show her with a tiny image of Amitābha in her hair.

You then repeat the refuge formula for the Buddha, Dharma, and Sangha, though in Tantric meditation these are given a Tantric flavour which varies according to the type of practice you are doing. In the Tārā practice, you consider Tārā herself as the Buddha; in other words, you take refuge in the compassion aspect of Enlightenment. Then the Dharma, in this practice, is Tārā's great compassion, as it is the compassion aspect of the Dharma with which you are particularly concerned. The Sangha in this context consists of the twenty-one manifestations or forms of Tārā. So you go for Refuge to Amitābha as the guru, to Tārā herself as the Buddha, to her compassion as the Dharma, and to her twenty-one forms as the Sangha. The same kind of pattern occurs in other practices. For example, if you were doing the Manjuśrī practice you would go for Refuge to Vairocana as the guru, to Manjuśrī as the Buddha, to his wisdom as the Dharma, and to his eight forms as the Sangha.

The second stage of the Green Tārā practice is the development of the four *brahma vihāras*, the four divine abodes or sublime states of mind. These are *maitrī*, that is, love in the sense of universal friendliness; *karuṇā*, compassion for all who suffer; *muditā*, sympathetic joy, in other words rejoicing in the happiness of others; and *upekṣā*, peace and equanimity of mind. The *brahma vihāras* are also found in the Mahāyāna and Hīnayāna, but in the Hīnayāna they are seen only as *śamathā* practices, that is, as having simply the function of calming the mind. In the Mahāyāna they are also considered to be *vipaśyanā* practices, means of developing

Insight, because when you develop these four sublime emotions and direct them towards all living beings, you realize at the same time that these beings are ultimately void or *śūnya*. This stage of the Tārā practice is seen as recapitulating the Mahāyāna in a Tantric context.

The next stage of the practice is the meditation on *śūnyatā* itself, also carried over from the Mahāyāna, where in fact it is seen as the main concern of meditation. This stage is extremely important. It is said that without some experience of voidness, some taste of *śūnyatā*, there is no real practice of the Vajrayāna. Yogi Chen, a friend and teacher of mine in Kalimpong, used to say that without the *śūnyatā* meditation, all the visualizations and rituals of the Vajrayāna are nothing but vulgar magic. Without the *śūnyatā* experience, your practice remains merely on the psychological level.

Fourthly there is the visualization of the bīja, in other words of the seed syllable of Tārā. In the background, as it were, there is *śūnyatā*, the Absolute, the Unconditioned, visualized as a deep blue sky; then in the midst of this you visualize the seed syllable. Every Tantric deity has a seed syllable of his or her own which is regarded as constituting the heart or essence of the deity. Just as a whole tree is contained, potentially, in a seed, the Buddha or Bodhisattva is contained in the bīja. Green Tārā's bīja is the syllable *tāṁ*. You visualize – in the midst of the void – this seed syllable, green in colour, in Tibetan or Sanskrit letters, standing upright on a horizontal moon disc on a white lotus, and radiating light in all directions.

Next we come to the central stage in the whole practice, the visualization of Green Tārā herself. She appears out of the seed syllable, green of course, with a beautiful smiling expression and wearing a crown ornamented with the five Buddhas, representing the five wisdoms. Her right hand rests on her right knee, palm outwards, representing generosity. Her other hand is held near her heart and holds a blue lotus with three blossoms which represent the Buddhas of the past, present, and future. One of her legs is folded in meditation posture, while the other hangs loose as though ready to step down. This symbolizes the fact that although immersed in meditation, in the experience of the Absolute, she is at the same time always ready to enter into the world to help people, out of compassion. Sometimes Green Tārā is said to embody three feminine archetypes: the virgin in the complete purity of her transcendental nature; the mother, in her love and compassion; and the queen, in her spiritual sovereignty and power.

There are different types or levels of visualization – in dreams or hallucinations one is visualizing – but the visualized image which one gets in meditation at this level should have a different quality. The visualized form of Tārā should not be solid and opaque, which would indicate a lower level of meditation. It should be visualized as delicate and diaphanous, like the colours of a rainbow. Or, as it is sometimes said, the colours should be seen like reflections in a mirror, quite evanescent and subtle.

Visualization plays an extremely important part in Tibetan Buddhist meditation. Generally speaking, its aim is to enable you to project from the depths of your mind higher aspects of yourself of which you are not as yet aware. The visualized image, in this case Tārā, acts as a focus for the corresponding qualities in you which are as yet undeveloped, but which are present in the unconscious. Tārā, representing compassion, becomes a focal point, at the level of the conscious or even supraconscious mind, for your own unrealized capacity for compassion. By means of the visualized image, these undeveloped feelings of compassion deep within you, which represent the higher part of your own nature, are enabled to cross the threshold of awareness and to be integrated into your conscious being at ever higher levels. To put it simply, through doing the Tārā visualization practice you become more compassionate yourself.

The sixth stage of the practice consists of the visualization and repetition of the Green Tārā mantra. In the heart of the visualized image of Tārā you see the seed syllable, *tāṁ*, and around it the ten letters of her mantra. You visualize these letters standing up vertically, emitting light and revolving in an anti-clockwise direction. (In the case of male deities the rotation is clockwise.) This is the most difficult part of the visualization, a stationary image being easier to see than one in motion. It is said that if you are mentally restless, you should visualize the letters of the mantra going round slowly, but that if you are feeling sluggish and sleepy they should be made to revolve briskly. As you visualize the letters going round, you repeat the mantra to yourself at least 108 times – the more the better. In between periods of meditation practice you can of course recite the mantra as often as you like.

In the next stage you dissolve the figure of Tārā, including the seed syllable and the mantra, back into the voidness, the 'blue sky', on which it has been superimposed. This is done gradually. You dissolve Tārā back into the lotus and 'moon mat' on which she sits, fade that into the mantra and then into the seed syllable, and finally allow the seed syllable to disappear into the voidness. This stage signifies the truth that all these forms, Buddhas or Bodhisattvas, Tārā or Manjuśrī or whoever, emerge from the void, from the depths of the 'One Mind', and do not exist apart from that. In other traditions it is often thought that the gods, goddesses, saints, sages, saviours, and so on appearing in meditation have a separate, objective existence of their own. But in Buddhism, in the Tantra, it is recognized that such forms and images are the products, ultimately, of one's own mind or consciousness, indeed of absolute mind itself. We impress this truth upon ourselves by dissolving the figure of Tārā back into the void from which she came.

Then the ninth stage consists of the double meditation of Tārā and the voidness. Here there is no build-up: the figure of Tārā appears instantaneously, like the silvery scales of a fish suddenly catching the light as it leaps from the water. Tārā springs up against the voidness, and you visualize the figure and experience the voidness at the same time. So far in the practice Tārā and the void have been concentrated on separately, but here you focus on their interpenetration, representing the identity of *rūpa* or form – represented here by Tārā – and *śūnyatā*. As the *Heart Sūtra* says, whatever is form, that is void, and whatever is void, that is form: there is no difference between them. In this stage you realize the truth of the *Heart Sūtra's* teaching. You realize, through actual experience, that the noumenal and the phenomenal, the Absolute and the relative, are not different. They are one. In this stage you also identify yourself and all other beings with Tārā, and you identify anything you hear with the mantra. If someone says something, you try to feel that this is Tārā herself speaking, this is the mantra of Tārā resounding. In this way, identifying yourself and all other beings with Tārā, you become yourself an embodiment of compassion.

The tenth and last stage of the practice is the dedication of merits, which is the conclusion to all Buddhist spiritual practices. Whatever merits you might have gained from this meditation practice, you resolve to share them with all living beings. There is nothing that you want to keep back for yourself.

This description gives at least some idea of the nature of the meditation on Green Tārā, but in order really to understand what it represents, what the experience involves, one has to practise it oneself. There is no other way to grasp what it is all about. The above description is only the meditation side of the practice – there are also ritual elements – but the whole thing is still quite simple by Tibetan standards. However, many ordinary practitioners, especially lay people, simplify it even further. They keep in their room, or on their shrine, an image or painted scroll of

Tārā, to give them an idea of what they should try to visualize. Then every morning they lay out seven offering bowls and fill them with water, usually repeating the mantra, and they light a lamp and some incense, perhaps looking at the image or bowing to it as they do so. This usually suffices for the ritual part of the practice. Then they sit down cross-legged on a rug on a sort of plank bedstead, and start the practice.

They start by reciting what we might call hymns, praising Tārā and her great compassion. Usually in these hymns she is described almost limb by limb, ornament by ornament, so that one can build up a picture of her in one's mind. Then they recite verses expressing their Going for Refuge, their practice of the four *brahma vihāras* and their taking of the Bodhisattva vow. And then just sitting there, perhaps looking at the picture and trying to see the image of Tārā in their minds, they go on repeating the Tārā mantra for half an hour or however long they can spare. They conclude by bowing down and dedicating their merits. This is how the ordinary person would do the practice. But if you are serious, especially if you have two or three hours to spare in the morning before you go to work, then you can go through the whole procedure.

These practices can certainly take some time to do. I remember, in connection not with the Tārā practice but with another one, that after the initiation I was given two written versions of the practice. My teacher said, 'Here's the short version, to be done every day, and here's a longer version for when you have two or three days to spare.' (Here he handed me twenty pages of instructions.) The Tārā practice is very commonly done among Tibetans, both monks and lay people. As they get older, as they have fewer and fewer responsibilities in the world, they devote more and more time to it, until eventually they may end up spending the greater part of the day in this way, not just with this particular practice but with a sequence of different practices. When I used to go and see my Tibetan friends in Kalimpong, very often I would arrive in the morning and the servant or disciple would say 'Please wait a few minutes, he hasn't quite finished his meditation.' After a while I learned that they usually started at about six in the morning and would finish at around nine. Whether they were government officials, or busy abbots in charge of monasteries, or just ordinary people, they would often spend two to three hours on their meditation and devotional practice before starting the day's work.

You would often see people reciting their mantras during the day, especially during their evening walk. One of my most pleasant memories of Kalimpong is of going for an evening stroll in the direction of the bazaar, and seeing, on the way, elderly Tibetan men and women walking along the road with a prayer wheel in one hand and a rosary in the other, murmuring mantras as they went. Western writers on Tibet have talked of rituals being performed mechanically, but there was nothing mechanical about this sort of practice. You could tell by the way people were concentrating that they were completely absorbed in what they were doing. In this way, even the comparatively advanced practices of Tantric Buddhist meditation could become an integral part of the daily life of the average Tibetan.

ཨོཾ་མ་ཎི་པདྨེ་ཧཱུྃ། ཨོཾ་མ་ཎི་པདྨེ་ཧཱུྃ། ཨོཾ་མ་ཎི་པདྨེ་ཧཱུྃ།
ཨོཾ་མ་ཎི་པདྨེ་ཧཱུྃ། ཨོཾ་མ་ཎི་པདྨེ་ཧཱུྃ། ཨོཾ་མ་ཎི་པདྨེ་ཧཱུྃ།

8

The Future of Tibetan Buddhism

In the preceding chapters we have surveyed a rich and dramatic field, and covered a great deal of ground. We have looked at both the distant past and more recent times. Surely anyone would be inspired by the great traditions and spiritual disciplines of Tibetan Buddhism, and the organization of the whole country around its religion. Other countries have tended to gear their national life to commerce or politics, to conquest or the arts, but in Tibet, the whole of life – political, economic, social, and artistic – has been focused on religion, on the Dharma. So for Buddhists, particularly, there is much to wonder at, admire, and learn from in the past of Tibetan Buddhism. But what is its future?

Having asked this question, we might as well face the unpalatable facts of the matter at once. As far as one can see, Tibetan Buddhism has no future. This great tradition of Buddhism, in its fullness, as it has existed in Tibet for hundreds of years, has had its day. In Tibet itself there are many ancient prophecies about the future of Tibetan Buddhism, and one which is often quoted by Tibetans is to the effect that the fourteenth Dalai Lama will be the last of his distinguished line. Tibetans who were well versed in the history and traditions of their country were, therefore, not altogether surprised when in 1959 the Dalai Lama had to flee from Tibet and seek shelter as a refugee in India. Unfortunate and tragic though it was, they knew that it had been prophesied that the fourteenth Dalai Lama would be the last. And it is not as if everything else in Tibet can remain the same except that there will no longer be a Dalai Lama. This is impossible. When the queen bee has gone, the life of the hive cannot continue. The Dalai Lama is central to the system. He summarizes or embodies in his person the whole of Tibetan Buddhism, and if he goes – and the prophecy does seem likely to be fulfilled – then the whole way of life which he represents will come to an end.

Tibet has been under Chinese domination since 1950, a year I remember very vividly. I had arrived in Kalimpong in March, and all summer there were rumours of war from the borderlands between Tibet and China. We heard that the Chinese armies were on the march, that they were building roads and bringing up reinforcements. First they entered Kham in eastern Tibet; we heard that monasteries had fallen, that monks had been massacred. And then week by week, month by month, we watched almost breathless as they advanced ever nearer and nearer to the sacred city of Lhasa. When the Chinese communists eventually reached Lhasa, many people felt that the end of an epoch had come.

The Chinese have been in Tibet ever since – time enough for a couple of generations to have grown up there – and many changes have taken place. In material terms there have been some improvements: roads have been laid down, hospitals built, schools opened. There have also been great psychological changes in the outlook of the Tibetan people, especially the young. This is due partly, no doubt, to Maoist indoctrination, but also to the inevitable march of time. The industrial revolution – to which Asia has largely succumbed – has at last caught up with Tibet. In some outlying areas of the country, within living memory they didn't even have the wheel. People can live perfectly well without wheels, but technologically it meant that not very long ago parts of Tibet were still in the Stone Age. Now they have the wheel in some of its most complex forms – they have cars and aircraft. Tibet, we may say, is one of the last major traditional civilizations to have yielded to the onrush of industrialization.

This has resulted in a tremendous culture shock, whose force it is difficult for us to appreciate. Suppose you were living, say at the time of the Norman Conquest, in your village, with your priest, with your farm work, and so on. And suppose suddenly, by some miracle, you were snatched up from the middle of the eleventh century and set down in the middle of the twentieth. You can imagine the shock you would experience on seeing everything so changed, so industrialized and mechanized.

In a way this is what has happened to many Tibetans. They've been lifted up from a very simple, albeit spiritually profound, civilization, and landed right in the middle of the twentieth century, exposed to all the technological and materialistic winds that blow. In many ways it is a very great pity that the traditional culture of Tibet has been disrupted and broken up in this way – but we can be pretty sure that it would have happened anyway, even if the Chinese had not invaded. The process might have been less dramatic, but it would inevitably have occurred.

In Kalimpong I often met young refugees fresh from Tibet. You could always spot the new arrivals because they would look around and take notice of things that others took for granted. The first time I took a party of my Tibetan students to Darjeeling, I remember how fascinated they were by the station and the railway engine. They were all men of about forty, but they were newly arrived, and hadn't seen a locomotive before. To them it was like an iron dragon, a great monster standing by the platform. In fact it was a tiny engine – the railway which goes up to the hills is called the 'Himalayan toy railway' – but they were very impressed by it. As they excitedly peered at it and underneath it, tapping the wheels and gesticulating to each other, suddenly it let out a loud hoot, and they sprang back in alarm as if they thought it might bite them.

When they first arrived in Kalimpong, most of the refugees – some of them aged only eighteen or twenty – looked typically Tibetan. They wore their hair long, as Tibetan men traditionally do, tied into a braid around their heads. Often they'd wear an earring, usually of turquoise, and they'd be wearing a chuba and tall boots. And of course they'd each have a mala or rosary in their hand. Now Kalimpong is just a quiet little town of 15,000 inhabitants, and rather backward by Western standards. Not everybody has electricity or running water. You wouldn't think there was much there to corrupt the innocent young Tibetan. But if you just waited six months and then took another look at those same Tibetans you'd find they had completely changed. They'd have cut off their long hair – that usually went first – and they'd be wearing sharkskin suits. They'd have given up their rosary, and you'd see them carrying around a transistor radio – you'd find them listening to pop music and wanting to learn to disco-dance. These were young men who six months before had been living in the Middle Ages. The women, incidentally, even the young women, were much more conservative. They might give up their malas and prayer wheels, but you didn't often see them cutting their hair or changing their dress.

We can't blame the Chinese communists for all the changes in Tibet itself and among the Tibetans in exile. This is the march of time. It may not be progress – I'm sure that in many ways it is not progress – but such changes are inevitable. Even if the Chinese had not come, Tibet would eventually have undergone this sort of process. So even if Tibet does succeed, as one hopes it will, in regaining independence, and the Dalai Lama returns and takes up residence again in the Potala, it will nevertheless be impossible to put the clock back. Tibet will never be again what it was for so many hundreds of years. It is in this sense that we can say that Tibetan Buddhism has no future.

This is a very great loss, no doubt, but perhaps we shouldn't be too shocked. All Buddhists know that the law of impermanence – *anitya* – governs and controls all human affairs, and the institutional forms of Buddhism itself are no exception. Buddhism began in India, where the Buddha lived and taught, and Indian Buddhism endured for 1,500 years; but in the end it disappeared. Nowadays, apart from modern revivals, we find little trace of Buddhism in India. So we should not be surprised if Buddhism were to disappear from Tibet after a similar period.

This does not mean that no vestige of Tibetan Buddhism will remain. As the way of life of a whole nation it has already come to an end, and I do not believe there can be any question of its revival. But Tibetan Buddhism will survive among the Tibetan refugees, in India and elsewhere, and it will survive as an integral part of Buddhism in the West.

Most Tibetan refugees – about 100,000 altogether – are found in India, mainly in the hill areas. Tibetans, coming from a very high country, understandably haven't been very happy in the hot plains of India. As far as possible they have clung to the hills, settling in places like Darjeeling, Kalimpong, and Sikkim, as well as in various parts of the Punjab and the Himachal Pradesh. There are also some Tibetans in Europe, especially in Switzerland, which houses the largest Tibetan refugee community outside India.

For refugees everywhere, the first question is that of physical survival. For many of the Tibetan refugees it has been a difficult business just to scrape a living. But as conditions improve they can begin to take steps to preserve their culture and their form of Buddhism. Tibetan temples and monasteries have been built in several places – for example, the two Tantric colleges have been re-opened in Dalhousie – and temples and monasteries have been built elsewhere in the foothills of the Himalayas. Handicraft centres have been opened by the refugees, producing paintings, carpets, metalwork, woodwork, and so on, along traditional lines –

albeit with some corruption in the matter of colour and design. So there is no doubt that Tibetan Buddhism, in some form, will survive in exile.

In time its position in India will probably be rather like that of Zoroastrianism among the Parsis of Bombay. The Parsis are a flourishing Indian community whose ancestors fled from Persia (now Iran) about 1,000 years ago, at the time of the Muslim invasion. It was a question of being converted to Islam or perishing, and a number of Zoroastrians, followers of the ancient teaching of the Persian prophet Zoroaster, decided to flee. They came by sea to the area which is now Bombay, and the Indians received them kindly, as the Indians usually do receive refugees. They were given land, settled down, and engaged in trade, and now are the richest communities in the whole of India. There are around 70,000 Parsis, and as a community they are enterprising, highly educated, and very charitable – they have endowed many schools and hospitals in Bombay. Above all, they preserve their ancient Zoroastrian faith which has virtually disappeared from its homeland.

Something like this is likely to happen with regard to Tibetan Buddhism in India. No doubt it will be preserved among the Tibetans in exile, especially as the refugee community includes many monks of all grades. But in Tibet itself, if the Chinese communists remain in power for a few more generations, it is very likely that Tibetan Buddhism will entirely disappear. We may not like to think that a religion can be wiped out, but it can. Manichaeism, the teaching of the prophet Mani – a sort of universalist, all-embracing religion – was at one time practised right across Europe and Asia, from France to China. But now it just doesn't exist. It was a very inoffensive faith – it believed in complete non-violence, in love and compassion – but it was stamped out by Persian kings, by the Roman Catholic Church, and by Chinese emperors. So we shouldn't think that Tibetan Buddhism is so great, so glorious, that it can't be wiped out in Tibet.

In fact, the decline of Tibetan Buddhism would seem to be part of a general trend in the East. All over Asia, it would appear, Buddhism is capitulating. China is lost to Buddhism, to all intents and purposes. Communism has virtually destroyed Buddhism in Mongolia and several countries of South-east Asia. Thai Buddhism is vulnerable to the march of Westernization. Japan is threatened not from without but from within, by over-industrialization; Buddhism does still exist there, but not as it did in the past. And in other parts of the East, Islam swept Buddhism away several hundred years ago. Just because the East was Buddhist for 2,000 years clearly does not mean it always will be. As far as we can see, in all the Buddhist countries of the East, Buddhism is in retreat, if not actually vanquished. It might seem a fantastic thought, but it may be that one day there will be very little Buddhism in the East and it will be stronger in the West. Bigger changes than this have taken place in world history.

But this is not the only reason why it is important for us in the West to study, to practise, and if possible to preserve Tibetan Buddhism. It is equally important that it should survive to become an integral part of Western Buddhism – indeed, of world Buddhism. Many different forms of Buddhism have been introduced into the West and are gradually spreading across the Western world, and it is already evident that Western Buddhism will not follow any one Eastern tradition exclusively. Sometimes Buddhists from the East are hopeful that their particular brand of Buddhism will take root in the West, and that all Western Buddhists will be strict Theravādins, or staunch followers of Sōtō Zen. But as far as we can see, this is not going to happen. It is certainly not happening at present. Western Buddhism is learning, and will continue to learn, from all the different oriental traditions of Buddhism as they become known. But people in the West will try to extract the essence of the teaching, the Buddha's real message, from all these different and differing traditions, and this ultimate and vital element in the teaching will be adapted to meet the psychological and spiritual needs of Western people.

In the West, people who are interested in religion and philosophy are weary of orthodoxies, weary of too much importance being placed on things which are not necessary, even quite unrelated to the essence of the teaching. Westerners who turn to any spiritual teaching emanating from the East are too much concerned with ultimate issues, with real human problems, to waste their time on the inessentials and trappings that have been handed down by the various Eastern Buddhist traditions. Much of what passes for Buddhism in the East has no connection with the teaching whatever. In Myanmar (Burma), for instance, there has been a bitter dispute as to whether when monks go out from the monastery, they should have the left shoulder covered and the right uncovered, or whether they should cover both shoulders. This dispute dominated the Burmese monastic community for a whole century and it is still not settled. Eastern Buddhists are often excessively preoccupied with such trivial matters; but such preoccupations are not going to go down very well in the West.

What we need is to encounter and get to grips with the essence of the Buddha's teaching, which is basically concerned with nothing other than the way to Enlightenment, mainly through ever-increasing awareness. This is what the Buddha was really talking about, and it is reflected and echoed in all the various traditions in different ways. It is to this essential theme that we need to pay attention, trying to adapt it to our own lives and to the lives of those around us. Which is not to say that in adapting the teaching there can be any question of compromising it or watering it down. On the contrary, we are concerned with the effective communication of the fundamental principles of the Dharma.

Tibetan Buddhism is just one of the forms of Buddhism with which we are currently becoming acquainted in the West. The main question we need to ask ourselves is: what can we learn from it? As we have seen, we can learn about Buddhism in general from its Tibetan form, by coming to understand how Buddhist teaching is reflected in Tibetan Buddhism. In this way one tradition can be a key to understanding the whole teaching. But we can also learn things which we may not learn from any other form of Buddhism, because Tibetan Buddhism is in many respects unique.

First of all, it represents Indian Buddhism at the height of its development. As we saw in Chapter 2, after 1,500 years Indian Buddhism was very rich and many-sided, including all three yānas, and it was this form of Buddhism which went from India to Tibet and was preserved there. So Tibetan Buddhism is the nearest we can get to Indian Buddhism as it was practised. It is all very well to read about ancient traditions in books, but it is much better to have some sort of contact, however indirect, with living traditions. Tibetan Buddhism is still a living tradition, albeit on a reduced scale, and it is our nearest contact with Indian Buddhism at its peak.

Dr Edward Conze had a rather interesting theory in this connection. He maintained that the nearer one is to the geographical centre of a religion, the nearer one is to its spirit. Tibet, Conze says, is closer geographically to the original centre of Buddhism than any other Buddhist country; and Tibetan Buddhism is therefore nearest to the spirit of Indian Buddhism. Whatever the merits of Conze's theory, it is certainly true that the spirit of Tibetan Buddhism seems remarkably close to that of Indian Buddhism during the last stages of its development in north-eastern India.

We can also learn from Tibetan Buddhism about all three yānas, not as unrelated paths, as it were side by side, but as aspects of a single path.

The idea that the Hīnayāna, Mahāyāna, and Vajrayāna are not just different forms of Buddhism but successive stages on the path to Enlightenment is a major feature of Tibetan Buddhism. It is first mentioned in the *Hevajra Tantra*, and it is worked out in greater detail by Atīśa in his *Bodhipatha Pradīpa* or 'Lamp of the Way to Enlightenment'. This doctrine is also the basis of Tsongkhapa's *Lam-rim chen-mo* or 'Great Stages of the Path'. All Tibetan Buddhist schools teach that one progresses to Enlightenment through a course of training in which one recapitulates in one's own practice the historical sequence of the three yānas. This triyāna synthesis is not found elsewhere in the Buddhist world. In South-east Asia we find only the Theravāda, a form of the Hīnayāna. In China or Japan we find both Hīnayāna and Mahāyāna (and here and there the Outer Tantra, though the Inner Tantra is found only in Tibet), but they are usually constituted into mutually exclusive, even rival, schools. Japanese Buddhism is more sectarian than any other Buddhist tradition. It is only in Tibet that we find all three yānas existing not as separate sects, but as stages of the one path leading to Enlightenment.

Tibetan Buddhism is also perhaps the most intellectual form of Buddhism that we know today. Although Tibetans in some areas did not even have the wheel until recently, this does not mean that they were primitive or uncultured, and it certainly does not mean that they were stupid. Intelligence and understanding, in the real sense, are not necessarily correlated with technological or material sophistication. Tibet has been the only part of the Buddhist world which has kept alive the highly intellectual tradition of Indian Buddhist logic.

Moreover, the exegesis of the Prajñāpāramitā, the Perfection of Wisdom tradition, was continued and even elaborated in Tibet. The Perfection of Wisdom sūtras are among the grandest and most sublime in the whole field of Buddhist canonical literature. They were produced in India and went to all the other Buddhist countries of the Far East, especially China and Japan. But it was only in Tibet that they continued to be studied, and that there was a tradition of teaching and explanation of the Prajñāpāramitā.

In this connection I remember hearing Edward Conze relate how when he was in the USA he met a lama of the Sakya School, which is renowned for its learning. Dr Conze had devoted some thirty years of his life to studying and translating the Perfection of Wisdom sūtras, and he had been doing this more or less on his own. This was no mean task – it required tremendous understanding, much knowledge and scholarship.

But there were just a few knotty points that even Conze could not clear up by himself.

So one day he went to see this lama and put some of these points to him. Whereupon the lama started explaining and expounding, and after he had been going on for a couple of hours, Conze was overwhelmed. 'I felt', he told me, 'that I really knew nothing about the Perfection of Wisdom. I became aware that there were vast stores of knowledge on the subject, the existence of which I hadn't even suspected.' And Dr Conze, it should be noted, was not given to handing out compliments. Quite the contrary, in fact. But this was his response to the Sakya lama, and it testifies to the tremendous intellectual tradition of the exegesis of the Prajñāpāramitā in Tibet.

At the same time, Tibetan Buddhism is highly devotional. All Tibetan Buddhists, including the learned geshes who are immersed in logic and the Perfection of Wisdom, have strong feelings of devotion for the Three Jewels. They have developed the intellect, perhaps as far as is humanly possible – but not one-sidedly. Their devotional side is also evident in all sorts of ways. One notices it in the way Tibetans handle images of Buddhas or Bodhisattvas. They do so very reverently, often putting them to their heads as a gesture of respect. Similarly with the sacred texts; it is unthinkable to Tibetans to fling a book on the floor. They consider that to be disgraceful, especially where the sacred scriptures are concerned – and most of their books are sacred scriptures. In fact in Tibetan Buddhism, whether among ordinary Buddhists or learned monks and abbots, the intellectual and emotional aspects of the religious life are not really divided at all. Their intense intellectuality is combined with profound devotion and faith. This is something else that we can learn from Tibetan Buddhism.

We find a similar balance in Tibetan Buddhism between study and meditation. Some of the most learned men in the Buddhist world are or were to be found among the geshes and lamas of Tibet, whose knowledge is often encyclopaedic. I remember once going to see Jamyang Khyentse Rimpoche, from whom I received certain initiations. He was very interested in various aspects of Indian literature, and in the course of conversation he suddenly asked me, through an interpreter, 'Do you know anything about dancing?' I said, 'Well, no, not really,' wondering what he was getting at. He went on to say: 'I've read fourteen books on Indian classical dance and there are a few points I want to clear up.' He had come from a remote corner of eastern Tibet, and here he was studying texts on Indian dance in Tibetan translation – they were in the Tangyur – and wanting to clear up some queries. I subsequently learned that these texts were the basis of the famous 'lama dances', which he was very interested in, and I believe later he did procure some treatises on the subject. He was exceptional, even among Tibetan lamas, but they all typically have such many-sided interests.

At the same time, these monks and lamas included some of the greatest yogis and meditators in the Buddhist world. Perhaps the most remarkable example is Milarepa, Tibet's greatest yogi and also her greatest poet, but there are many instances in Tibetan Buddhism of this type of person – great scholars, with wonderful intellectual knowledge, who are at the same time profound meditators, understanding not only the theory but also the practice of the spiritual life. Jamyang Khyentse was himself of this type. He was by no means a 'dry-as-dust' bookworm. When he was not studying he was meditating, and he was famous for both. It's rather as if someone like Bertrand Russell was also a sort of St John of the Cross. To our Western way of thinking, this kind of combination is extraordinary, it breaks all the rules. We don't find it even in the Christian tradition in the Middle Ages. St Thomas Aquinas was a great scholar and theologian; it was only towards the end of his life that he turned to mysticism, and then, rather significantly, he gave up theology. St Francis, on the other hand, was a great spiritual soul, but he probably knew nothing about theology. But in Tibetan Buddhism we often find, combined in one person, the genius of the scholar and the simplicity and spiritual experience of the mystic.

This balanced approach is something else that we can learn from Tibetan Buddhism, not only in respect of intellect and faith, or study and meditation, but also in less important areas. In Tibetan Buddhism we find a combination of organization and freedom, two things which in the West we usually consider antithetical. Tibet had the biggest monasteries in the world, yet at the same time it had the loneliest, most isolated hermitages. There were monasteries with thousands of monks, but you could also go hundreds of miles out into the wilderness and find a cave, a shack, or a little temple with just one solitary hermit living in it.

There was another synthesis: of highly organized monasticism on the one hand and serious spiritual practice by lay people on the other. In a way, Tibetan Buddhism was the most monasticized in the world. There were monks everywhere. Just imagine walking down Oxford Street in London and finding that every other person you met was a monk. This is what it was like in Lhasa in the old days. Wherever you went there were monks. You might even think that they were rather monk-ridden.

But although monks constituted a higher percentage of the population in Tibet than in any other country in the world, at the same time there was full participation by the laity in the spiritual life. No one thought that you had to be a monk in order to practise the Dharma. In fact, among the Nyingmapas the laity, including the lay lamas, practically ran the show. In Theravādin countries they tend to think that you can't be a real Buddhist unless you become a monk; but in Tibet, though they had so many monks, they never thought like this.

To generalize even more, one may say that while Tibetan Buddhists have their head in the clouds, at the same time their feet are firmly on the ground. They try to follow the most sublime and rarefied of all spiritual ideals – that of the Bodhisattva, one who does not care for his or her own individual salvation but who is devoted to the spiritual welfare of all beings. This is their ideal, which everyone appreciates and to some extent tries to follow. At the same time the Tibetans are intensely practical in all affairs of life, whether it is to do with food, or clothing, or building, or making money in trade and business. We might go so far as to say that there's nothing mystical, nothing occult about the Tibetans at all, not in the woolly sense of those terms. Westerners have often tended to think of the Tibetans as wonderful mystical figures, living beyond the Himalayas in an aura of mystery, surrounded by all sorts of strange happenings. The idea that Tibetans ever thought of eating or drinking or making money was at one time almost blasphemy among some occult circles in the West, who would speak of 'the masters beyond the Himalayas' as if they were always immersed in meditation and never thought of anything else. But the Tibetans are not like this at all. They are mystical in the true sense. They have their heads in the clouds spiritually, but their feet are firmly planted on the earth. This is something we might emulate.

We can learn many other things from Tibetan Buddhism. For example, we can learn depth and sincerity. Tibetan Buddhists are remarkably sincere, in the full sense of that much-misused word. They really do believe in their religion. We can also strive to equal their thoroughness. It is very difficult to get Tibetans to commit themselves. If you ask them to do something, or to help in some way, they agree very slowly and reluctantly. They go through every step of it with you, making sure they understand exactly what you are asking them to do. Only then will they commit themselves and say 'Yes'; but when they have done so, you know you can depend on them. They are very thorough and reiiable. We can aspire to their strenuousness too. I have often heard Tibetans say that there is no religious life without difficulty. They tend to think that if any religious practice is easy it can't be truly religious. They believe that there are no easy ways round, no short cuts. They are prepared to endure hardship and suffering for the sake of their spiritual life. We saw in Chapter 1 how King Yeshe Ö of western Tibet sacrificed his life so that the Buddha's teaching might be revived in western Tibet.

We can therefore conclude that Tibetan Buddhism is a highly developed, fully articulated, balanced, and harmonious system of Buddhism. There is nothing one-sided in it. Moreover, we can say that it is the richest form of Buddhism, in the sense that, within its harmony and synthesis, it includes the greatest number of diverse elements. In the West we have perhaps only one form of religion which can compare with Tibetan Buddhism in respect of richness – and I'm only thinking of richness when I make the comparison – and that is Roman Catholicism. But there are of course many very weighty differences between them, and one respect in which they differ very much is that Tibetan Buddhism, unlike Roman Catholicism, is characterized by tolerance. Tolerance is characteristic of all forms of Buddhism, but one might think that the temptation to intolerance would be greater in Tibetan Buddhism inasmuch as its internal differences are greater. But it has not yielded to that temptation. The scholar does not look down upon the yogi, nor the yogi upon the scholar. There is no rivalry between the monks and the laity, but full co-operation. There are four schools, each proud of its own traditions and adhering to them faithfully, but they all display deep mutual courtesy. Their differences rarely degenerate into criticism, much less into hostility. In the course of all my contact with lamas of all schools I never heard from, say, a Nyingma lama a real criticism of the Gelug tradition, or vice versa. Of course they are human, and sometimes they have little jokes at each other's expense. I remember a Gelug joke about the Nyingma wong – the Tantric initiation – to the effect that the Nyingmapas had very powerful, esoteric wongs, such as they, the Gelugpas, didn't have: they even had a wong so powerful that you could give it to others without having practised it yourself. To appreciate the humour of this one has to understand the Tibetan attitude towards wongs; the point is that the joking is done in the friendliest spirit.

The tolerance of the Tibetans extends to non-Buddhists, and sometimes Tibetans are very shocked when they come to India and encounter Christian missionaries for the first time. They can hardly believe their ears. If they hear a Christian criticizing Buddhism, they see it as someone criticizing religion in any form, which *they* would never do. They are not averse to the free expression of religious differences, but in Tibetan

Buddhism such differences are always expressed courteously. I remember a young lama coming to see me shortly after the influx of refugees into Kalimpong in 1959 and telling me he had just discovered that communism and Christianity were the same thing. When I asked him what had led him to that conclusion, he explained that he had just heard some Christian missionaries preaching in the bazaar (as they did every week) and vigorously denouncing Buddhism and Hinduism. In Lhasa the young lama had heard Chinese communists denouncing Buddhism in exactly the same terms. So obviously communism and Christianity were the same thing.

Western Buddhists can learn a great deal from this. As a living religion, Buddhism in the West is very recent. At first we just had some Theravāda, then a little Mahāyāna was added, including Zen, and more recently we've come to know about Tibetan Buddhism, including the Tantra. Western Buddhism will not and should not be confined to any one of these traditions – it will be a synthesis of them all. But we do not want it to be just a jumble. Perhaps we can learn from Tibetan Buddhism how to achieve a harmonious synthesis of all the different elements in the total Buddhist tradition. Obviously this will not be achieved without mutual respect and tolerance, and this too we can learn from the Tibetans. We can't hope that all Buddhists in the West will see Buddhism in exactly the same way. We have to accept this, and work together nevertheless, reconciling our differences in the light of the one ideal, the one objective, which we all accept, which is Enlightenment or Buddhahood.

Nobody can say with any certainty what the future holds for Tibet. But we in the West have the opportunity to follow, however hesitatingly, in the footsteps of the Tibetans, who achieved in the past such a magnificent and rich synthesis of the total Buddhist tradition. If we can do this, then Western Buddhism, though it may be confined to comparatively few people, may become as rich and many-splendoured as was the Buddhism of Tibet.

Further Reading

Stephen Batchelor (ed.), *Resistance and Reform in Tibet*, Hurst & Co., London 1994

Stephen Batchelor, *The Tibet Guide*, Wisdom, London 1987

Stephen Batchelor (ed.), *The Jewel in the Lotus – a Guide to the Buddhist Traditions of Tibet*, Wisdom, London 1987

Alaka Chattopadhyaya, *Atīśa and Tibet*, Indian Studies Past and Present, Calcutta 1967

Melvyn C. Goldstein, *A History of Modern Tibet, 1913 – 1951: the Demise of the Lamaist State*, University of California Press, Berkeley 1989

Lama Anagarika Govinda, *Foundations of Tibetan Mysticism*, Weiser, York Beach Maine 1969

Lama Anagarika Govinda, *The Way of the White Clouds*, Rider, London 1995

Li Gotami Govinda, *Tibet in Pictures: A Journey into the Past* (2 vols.), Dharma, California 1979

Landaw and Weber, *Images of Enlightenment: Tibetan Art in Practice*, Snow Lion, Ithaca, New York 1993

John Powers, *Introduction to Tibetan Buddhism*, Snow Lion, Ithaca, New York 1995

David Snellgrove and Hugh Richardson, *A Cultural History of Tibet*, Shambhala, Boston/London 1986

Yeshe Tsogyal, *The Life and Liberation of Padmasambhava*, Dharma, California 1978

Index